REVISE EDEXCEL GCSE

History

Specification B Schools History Project

REVISION WORKBOOK

Extend

Authors: Nigel Bushnell and Cathy Warren

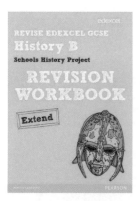

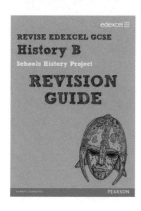

THE REVISE EDEXCEL SERIES

Available in print or online

Online editions for all titles in the Revise Edexcel series are available Autumn 2012.

Presented on our ActiveLearn platform, you can view the full book and customise it by adding notes, comments and weblinks.

Print editions

History B Extend Revision Workbook	9781446905074
History B Support Revision Workbook	9781446905104
History B Revision Guide	9781446905142

Online editions

History B Extend Revision Workbook	9781446905159
History B Support Revision Workbook	9781446904985
History B Revision Guide	9781446905166

Print and online editions are also available for History Specification A Support and Extend Workbooks and Revision Guide.

This Revision Workbook is designed to complement your classroom and home learning, and to help you prepare for the exam. It does not include all the content and skills needed for the complete course. It is designed to work in combination with Edexcel's main GCSE History 2009/2012 Series.

To find out more visit:
www.pearsonschools.co.uk/edexcelgcsehistoryrevision

ALWAYS LEARNING   PEARSON

Published by Pearson Education Limited, Edinburgh Gate, Harlow, Essex, CM20 2JE.

www.pearsonschoolsandfecolleges.co.uk

Text © Pearson Education Limited 2012
Designed and typeset by Juice Creative Limited, Hertfordshire and Jerry Udall
Cover illustration by Miriam Sturdee

The rights of Nigel Bushnell and Cathy Warren to be identified as authors of this work have been asserted
by them in accordance with the Copyright, Designs and Patents Act 1988.

First published 2012

16 15 14 13 12
10 9 8 7 6 5 4 3 2 1

British Library Cataloguing in Publication Data
A catalogue record for this book is available from the British Library

ISBN 978 1 446 90507 4

Printed in Slovakia by Neografia

Acknowledgements
Picture Credits
The publisher would like to thank the following for their kind permission to reproduce their photographs:

akg-images Ltd: Coll. F. Kunst & Geschichte 11; **British Library Images Online**: 7; **Corbis**: David
Pollack 70, Gideon Mendel 9, Peter Aprahamian 71; **John Bartlett**: 75; **Mary Evans Picture Library**:
Illustrated London News 72, Weimar Archive 13

All other images © Pearson Education

Written Sources
We are grateful to the following for permission to reproduce copyright material: Extract on page 74
adapted from `An account of the 1984 Miners' Strike', http://archiveshub.ac.uk/features/mar04.shtml.
Reproduced by kind permission of The South Wales Coalfield Collection, Swansea University.

Every effort has been made to contact copyright holders of material reproduced in this book. Any
omissions will be rectified in subsequent printings if notice is given to the publishers.

In order to ensure that this resource offers high-quality support for the associated Edexcel qualification,
it has been through a review process by the awarding organisation to confirm that it fully covers the
teaching and learning content of the specification or part of a specification at which it is aimed, and
demonstrates an appropriate balance between the development of subject skills, knowledge and
understanding, in addition to preparation for assessment.

While the publishers have made every attempt to ensure that advice on the qualification and its
assessment is accurate, the official specification and associated assessment guidance materials are the
only authoritative source of information and should always be referred to for definitive guidance.

No material from an endorsed revision workbook will be used verbatim in any assessment set by Edexcel.

Endorsement of a revision workbook does not mean that the revision workbook is required to achieve
this Edexcel qualification, nor does it mean that it is the only suitable material available to support the
qualification, and any resource lists produced by the awarding organisation shall include this and other
appropriate resources.

Contents

Introduction

This workbook has been written to help you practise your exam skills as you prepare for your GCSE History exams for Unit 1, Unit 2 and Unit 3. You'll find practice for each question type, helping you to understand what is required. You'll find answers to the activities at the back of the book, so that you can check whether you're on track after you've completed the activities.

Unit 1 Development Study and Unit 2 Depth Study

This workbook covers the following options for Unit 1 and Unit 2:

- 1A Medicine and treatment
- 1B Crime and punishment
- 2B The American West c.1840–c.1895
- 2C Life in Germany c.1919–c.1945

In these two units, the questions follow a similar pattern, testing similar key historical skills. For that reason in this workbook, we look at each historical skill and the Unit 1 and 2 questions that relate to it together. In the exam papers for both units, you will answer five questions.

Question 1	4 marks	Question 3 or Question 4	12 marks
Question 2	9 marks	Question 5(a) and 5(b) or Question 6(a) and 6(b)	(a) 9 marks and (b) 16 marks

In questions 5(b) and 6(b), there are additional marks for spelling, punctuation and grammar.

The examination paper

In both Unit 1 and Unit 2, the questions follow the same pattern.

You must do question 1, which is always an inference question worth 4 marks.

Question 2 is worth 9 marks and there is always a choice of two options within the question, for example:

You then choose EITHER question 3 or question 4. Each of these is worth 12 marks and they always have some stimulus material – a picture, a brief piece of text or 3 bullet points. This stimulus material is just to help you get started. It reminds you to cover the whole period, look at both sides of the issue, cover more than one factor and so on. However, you need to have enough knowledge to make use of this stimulus material: you can't just rewrite it in your own words. Ideally you will also add some additional points from your own knowledge.

There were two important developments in medical knowledge during the years 1500-1861. Choose ONE of the boxes below and explain why it was important.

Improvements in knowledge of anatomy

Pasteur's germ theory

You then choose EITHER question 5 or question 6. Whichever question you choose, you must answer part (a) AND part (b). Part (a) is worth 9 marks and is usually a straightforward question asking you to describe a situation or identify the key features. Part (b) is the evaluation question which is worth 16 marks.

Question	Marks	Suitable length of answer (exam booklet)	Time
1	4	8–10 lines	5–7 mins
2	9	1–1½ side	10–12 mins
3 or 4	12	1½ –2 sides	15–20 mins
5 or 6	Part (a) 9 Part (b) 16	Part (a) 1 side Part (b) 2–2½ sides	Part (a) 10 mins Part (b) 25 mins

In Unit 1, there are 3 additional marks for spelling, punctuation and grammar in question 5(b)/6(b). In Unit 2, there are 4 additional marks in question 5(b)/6(b). Remember to leave time at the end of the exam to check the quality of your writing.

Unit 3 Source Enquiry

This workbook covers the following options in Unit 3.

- 3A The transformation of surgery c.1845–c.1918
- 3B Protest, law and order in the twentieth century

You'll find the sources for option 3A on pages 68–69 and the sources for option 3B on pages 70–72. The questions and activities in this workbook will relate to those sources. There are five questions in Unit 3 and you should answer all five. The table below shows which source skill is being tested in each question as well as where you will be marked on your spelling, punctuation and grammar. On pages 65–67, each question type is explained, followed by the sources and the examples and activities for 3A and 3B.

Question 1	6 marks	Inference	Pages 73–78
Question 2	8 marks	Portrayal	Pages 73–78
Question 3	10 marks	Cross-referencing	Pages 79–83
Question 4	10 marks	Evaluation of sources	Pages 84–89
Question 5	16 marks + 3 marks	Reaching a judgement Spelling, punctuation and grammar	Pages 90–97

The examination paper

Unit 3 is slightly different. Each question focuses on a specific skill. You have no choice and you must answer all five questions.

Question	Marks	Suitable length of answer (exam booklet)	Time
1 Inference	6	$^2/_3$–1 side	5–7 mins
2 Portrayal	8	1 side	10 mins
3 Cross-referencing	10	2 sides	15–20 mins
4 Evaluation of sources	10	1½ sides	12–15 mins
5 Reaching a judgement	16	2–2½ sides	25–30 mins

Inference questions

The first question in both Unit 1 and Unit 2 is an **inference** question. An inference means something that is not actually stated or shown in the source but something you can work out from the details of the source.

How do I answer inference questions?

Unit 1 is a Development Study: it focuses on change and continuity over time. In Unit 1 you will therefore need to make an inference about **change**, based on **two** given sources.

In Unit 2, the Depth Study, you will need to make an inference from just **one** given source.

When answering the inference questions in Units 1 and 2, use only the source(s) given to you – you do not need to use any additional own knowledge.

How will I be marked?

The inference questions in both units are worth 4 marks and the mark scheme spreads the marks over two levels:

- Level 1 (1–2 marks): the answer makes an inference but without supporting detail from the source(s) OR the answer identifies relevant points from the source(s) but doesn't explain what inference has been made.

- Level 2 (3-4 marks): the answer makes an inference and supports it with details from the source(s).

So you need to look at the source(s) then make an inference AND support your inference by using details from the source(s).

Things to avoid!

Watch out for these common pitfalls:

- making an inference but not explaining which details of the source have been used

- describing details of the source but not saying what you have worked out (inferred) from these details

- writing too much – you're given 12 lines for your answer but really you shouldn't need more than 10 and some answers have scored full marks in only 5 lines. Remember – the more time you spend answering this question, the less time you'll have to answer the final question, which is worth 16 marks. Get to the point!

For the type of inference questions (question 1) that you will get in Unit 1, go to page 7 for Medicine or page 9 for Crime. For the type that you will get in Unit 2, go to page 11 for American West or page 13 for Life in Germany.

Unit 1 focuses on change and continuity over time. Therefore Unit 1 question 1 always asks you to make inferences about change. For example:

> What can you learn from Sources A and B about changes in nursing in the period between the Middle Ages and the start of the twentieth century? Explain your answer, using these sources. (4 marks)

Source A: An illustration from the Middle Ages, showing a housewife and her maid preparing medicine for the man lying ill in bed.

Source B: From a letter written by William Rathbone to Liverpool nurses in 1901.

> As nurses, you are not inferior servants doing inferior work for inferior wages, but trained and skilled workers carrying out intelligently the treatment prescribed by a doctor.

Activity

1. Look at the five comments below. Circle the letter(s) where the comment about changes in nursing is a valid one and has been based on the two sources above.

   a. Nurses were better trained as a result of the work of Florence Nightingale.

   b. Nursing used to be done by the women of the family but changed to be done by trained nurses.

   c. Nurses were respected more in the twentieth century than in the Middle Ages.

   d. Women acted independently, making their own medicines, during the Middle Ages but in the twentieth century they worked under the supervision of a doctor.

   e. Nursing used to be done at home but in the twentieth century it was only done in hospitals.

Read the example below that demonstrates how one of the comments has been turned into a Level 2 answer.

Answer A

Nursing used to be done by the women of the family, at home, as is shown in Source A where the man is in bed and the woman is sitting in front of the fire making her own medicine by following a recipe. By the twentieth century nursing had changed to something that was done by trained nurses, which is shown in Source B where Rathbone tells nurses they are 'not inferior servants ... but trained and skilled workers'.

2. Look again at the five comments about change and find the other comment that is based on the sources. Write two sentences that clearly identify the inference about change and support this comment by using a detail from each source.

....

....

Study Answer B below.

3. Underline in blue the details that come from the sources.

4. Underline in red the comment about change.

5. Use the mark scheme on page 6 to decide how many marks you would give it.

Answer B

In Source A, I can see a woman using a recipe book to prepare medicine for the man who is sick and is lying in bed and her maid is helping her. This shows the way that nursing in the Middle Ages was done in the home, by the women of the family, using their own remedies. In Source B, Rathbone is writing to several nurses. The fact that he talks about nurses carrying out treatment prescribed by a doctor suggests they are working in a hospital. He says that nurses had become 'trained and skilled workers'. This is because Florence Nightingale made a lot of changes to the training of nurses and made it a respectable thing to do. Rathbone seems to have a lot of respect for the nurses and this shows that nursing has changed by 1901 and has become a profession which is carried out in hospitals.

I would give this .... marks.

Now read the feedback below to see if you were right.

This does make an inference about changes in nursing and that inference is based on details from the sources so it is Level 2. However, the focus is on the detail in the sources, rather than the inference about change, so it would receive 3 marks rather than 4. The comment about Florence Nightingale is true but it is not based on the sources and therefore gets no marks. This answer also takes too long to get to the point.

6. Now create an improved answer by focusing on the **changes in nursing** and only including detail from the sources if it is being used to support your comment.

....

....

....

....

....

....

....

....

Unit 1 is a Development Study, focusing on change and continuity over time.
Therefore question 1 always asks you to make inferences about change. For example:

> What can you learn from Sources A and B about changes in riot control in the period from the eighteenth century to the end of the twentieth century? (4 marks)

Source A:
A proclamation by King George III in 1780 saying that the army will be used to deal with riots.

> A great number of people have gathered together in a riot. It has become necessary to use military force in order to deal with these disturbances, to protect the lives and properties of individuals, and to restore the peace of the country.

Source B: Police in riot gear controlling a demonstration in London in 1999.

Activity

1. Look at the five comments below. Circle the letter(s) where the comment is a valid one about changes in riot control and has been based on the two sources above.

   a. The army were used to control riots in the eighteenth century.

   b. The army used military force to control riots and were likely to injure or kill people whereas in Source B the police weapons are less likely to kill protesters.

   c. Robert Peel started the Metropolitan Police Force in 1829.

   d. Controlling riots and protecting property used to be treated as an emergency and done by the army but in the twentieth century it was done by the police who were trained to deal with riots as part of their normal duties.

   e. The police have protective clothing and shields but they are not attacking the protesters in an attempt to control them.

Read the example below that demonstrates how one of the comments has been turned into a Level 2 answer.

Answer A

The sources show a change in both the people and the methods used to control riots. Riot control used to be done by the army who would use military force and therefore were likely to be aggressive and injure or kill the protesters. By the twentieth century, the police were dealing with riots and they had been specially trained and equipped for riot control so that they did not use military force and were less likely to kill or injure protesters.

2. Look again at the five comments about change and find the other comment that is based on the sources. Write two sentences that clearly identify the change and support this comment by using a detail from each source.

....

....

Study Answer B below.

3. Underline in blue the details that come from the sources.

4. Underline in red the comment about change.

5. Use the mark scheme on page 6 to decide how many marks you would give it.

Answer B

In Source A, I can see that the army was used to deal with riots in the eighteenth century. They would attack the people in order to restore order and would probably injure or kill people. This shows that riot control in the eighteenth century was treated almost like a war and riots were controlled by violence. By the twentieth century, this has changed because the police dealt with riots and they were trained to avoid using violence. When the police were first introduced in the nineteenth century they wore a top hat and their coat was blue to make them look different from the army. In B the police have been trained to make a defensive wall to prevent the rioters going any further but they are not attacking them.

I would give this .... marks.

Read the feedback below to see if you were right.

This does make an inference about changes in riot control and that inference is based on details from the sources so it is Level 2. However, the focus is on the detail in the sources, rather than the inference about change, so it would receive 3 marks rather than 4. The comment about the police uniform in the nineteenth century is true but it is not based on the sources and therefore gets no marks. This answer also takes too long to get to the point.

6. Now create an improved answer by focusing on the **changes in riot control** and only including detail from the sources if it is being used to support your comment.

....

....

....

....

Unit 2 is a Depth Study which explores a short period of rapid change in history.
Here is an example of the type of inference question you will get for question 1 in Unit 2.

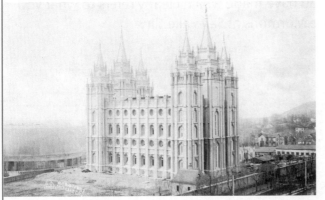

Source A: The Mormon Temple in Salt Lake City, 1895.

What can you learn from Source A about the Mormon settlement at Salt Lake City? (4 marks)

Hint

First it is useful to look at the caption. This tells you when the photograph was taken. This will help you to think about your answer because you now know that it was taken almost 50 years after the Mormons first arrived at the Great Salt Lake.

Activity

1. Which of the following are valid inferences that you could make from this particular source? Circle the correct answer(s).

   a. Many Mormons used the temple.

   b. It looks like there is a sense of pride in the city because it is well looked after.

   c. The Mormons had escaped religious persecution in the east.

   d. The size of the temple shows that religion was clearly important to the Mormons.

   e. Most of the people living in the city are rich.

Now you need to support your inference directly from the source you are using.

2. Read the statements below. For each one, tick the relevant column to show if it:

   A. can be used to support your inference made from this source

   B. is based on own knowledge but not from this source.

	A	B
1. The Mormons had a very skilful leader in Brigham Young.		
2. The temple shows the city was wealthy.		
3. The Mormons had escaped religious persecution in the east.		
4. The Mormon Church shared out land equally among the people.		
5. The Mormons encouraged others to join them by making funds available.		

3. Now write an answer to this question. Remember that the best answers:

○ make a clear inference from this source about the Mormons' success at Salt Lake City

○ make a statement to support the inference you have made which clearly refers to what you can see in the source about the success of the Mormons at Salt Lake City.

....

....

....

....

Read the two student answers A and B below.

Answer A

In Source A I can see that the Mormons were successful at Salt Lake City because the city looks well cared for. You can also tell that religion was important because of the large temple. A lot was achieved because of the skills shown by Brigham Young. The Mormons also encouraged many other people with useful skills to join them with the setting up of the Perpetual Emigration Fund. This encouraged others to join them from as far away as Europe. Brigham Young's success meant that the US government appointed him as governor for the new state of Utah.

Answer B

The Mormons used a variety of means to ensure that Salt Lake City was successful. The city had a large temple. From the centre of the city land was then shared out equally. The city was in the middle of the desert and they could not use water from the Salt Lake. However, the Mormons developed a system of irrigation which meant they could grow crops, as well as grow trees in the city.

4. Give a mark for each student's answer and explain why you have awarded that mark. Remember to use the mark scheme on page 6.

Answer A mark:	Answer B mark:
Explanation:	Explanation:

5. Student A has written too much for this question. Underline the parts of Answer A that are the only points needed for this question.

2C Life in Germany

Unit 2 is a Depth Study which explores a short period of rapid change in history.
Here is an example of the type of inference question you will get for question 1 in Unit 2.

Source A: A photograph of book-burning in central Berlin, May 1933

> What can you learn from Source A about the methods used by the Nazi government to control Germany? (4 marks)

Hint

First remember to look at the caption. This tells you when the photograph was taken. This will help you to think about your answer because you now know that it was taken in the period between Hitler becoming Chancellor and then Führer of Germany.

Activity

1. Which of the following are valid inferences which you could make from this particular source? Circle the correct answer(s).

    a. The Nazis were against the Jews and communists.

    b. The Nazis wanted to control what people read.

    c. The Nazis believed in expanding eastwards.

    d. Many Germans were against book burning.

    e. The Nazis wanted to destroy ideas and beliefs which they did not agree with.

Now you need to support your inference directly from the source you are using.

2. Read the statements below. For each one, tick the relevant column to show if it:

    A. can be used to support your inference made from this source

    B. is based on own knowledge but not from this source.

	A	B
1. Books were burnt as if it were a ceremony with people saluting Hitler.		
2. Books by Jewish authors were publicly burnt.		
3. Books were burnt openly in major towns and cities in full view of the public.		
4. Goebbels ordered the burning of books.		
5. The Nazi government also controlled films, plays and music.		

3. Now write an answer to this question. Remember that you need to:

- make a clear inference from the source about the Nazi government's methods of control

- make a statement to support the inference you have made which clearly refers to what you can see in the source about methods used by the Nazi government to control Germany.

....

....

....

....

Read the two student answers A and B below.

Answer A

From Source A I can see that one method used by the Nazis to control Germany was the burning of books which did not agree with the Nazi government's beliefs. These book-burnings were ordered by the Minister for Propaganda. This was done in busy areas in full public view. The burnings were almost like a ceremony or ritual to celebrate the Nazi government. This was part of the whole policy of censorship used by the Nazi government, which as well as books also included newspapers, films, radio, plays and music. By the late 1930s it was impossible for those who did not agree with the Nazis to publish or broadcast any of their materials.

Answer B

A method used by the Nazis to control Germany was to control ideas. They did this by using ways to stop ideas with which they did not agree from spreading. They also made sure that people only read and heard ideas that the Nazis believed in. One way of doing this was by burning books. This was organised by supporters of Hitler and was often like a ritual which celebrated the destruction of work that the Nazis wanted rid of – such as books by Jews and communists.

4. Assess each answer and explain your decision. Remember to use the mark scheme on page 6.

Answer A mark:	Answer B mark:
Explanation:	Explanation:

5. Student A has written too much for this question. Underline the parts of student A's answer that are the only points needed for this question.

Causation questions

Causation means looking at WHY things happen in history – the CAUSES of events and change. To answer a causation question you need to EXPLAIN why something happened.

How will I be marked?

In both Unit 1 and Unit 2, any question could ask about causation, except question 1. Questions 2, 5(a) and 6(a) are worth 9 marks, and questions 3 and 4 are worth 12 marks. However, they are all marked in the same way, using levels, going from Level 1 up to Level 3.

The best answers do the following things.

- Focus on EXPLANATION not description. So, rather than telling 'a story' by narrating the events, you need to explain WHY things happened. You can do this by using words or phrases such as 'because', 'therefore', 'as a result' and 'which meant that' to show connections between the points you are making in your answer.

- Group different reasons together. These might be:

  - economic factors (reasons to do with money)

  - political factors (reasons to do with power and authority)

  - religious factors (reasons to do with people's beliefs)

  - social factors (reasons to do with the way society works and people's attitudes).

- Show a range of causes. You should aim for three or four distinct points; depending on the question, this could mean three or four examples of economic consequences, or one example each of the economic, social and political causes.

We also sometimes identify the role of an individual factor, for example:

- the government (what decisions were made, what was organised on a national basis)

- technology (how equipment and machinery affected the situation)

- science (how new ideas affected people's understanding of events)

- war (how the situation of war affected events and people's lives).

In Other Words

If your teacher asked you why you were late for school you could say:

We had a power cut during the night so I got up late. There had also been an accident on the way to school.

This would be a Level 2 answer. it is a description and does not make clear the link between each point and being late. A Level 3 answer would organise the explanation, identify the role of technology (the alarm didn't go off) and chance (the accident).

Unit 1 is a Development Study. Questions on causation in this unit ask why change happened but also why change didn't happen (why there was continuity) or why it took so long for the situation to change. For example:

Why did it take so long for penicillin to be produced on a large scale? (12 marks)

The following information may help you with your answer.

Alexander Fleming investigated penicillin bacteria in 1928 when it affected a mould he was growing as part of an experiment. He published his findings in an article in 1929.

Activity

1. Study Answer A below. Underline any reasons it gives to explain why the mass production of penicillin did not happen in 1928.

Answer A

When Alexander Fleming found that a mould he had been growing in a petri dish was being killed off by a new bacteria growing there, he investigated and found that the new bacteria, penicillin, could kill other bacteria – it was an antibiotic which could be used to fight infection. He felt it only had limited use because he found that it was killed by stomach acid and therefore he thought it could only be used on the skin, not as medicine for illness. It was also difficult to produce in large quantities. He published his findings in a medical journal but then went back to his original research and no further work was done until Florey and Chain decided to investigate penicillin. They managed to purify it and found it was effective if injected into the bloodstream. They needed funding to mass produce it but the British government did not help. The American government was willing to fund their work because they knew that in the First World War more soldiers had died from infection than from the actual wounds they had received, so penicillin would help to keep their soldiers alive.

2. Read the feedback below, then complete the table on the next page to say whether each of the suggested changes would improve Answer A and, if so, why.

This answer is clearly Level 3 because it identifies several reasons why it took so long to mass produce penicillin but it presents them separately. It would be a top Level 3 answer if it showed how these reasons interacted with each other – for example, the fact that Fleming was working alone and on a different project limited the amount of time he could spend investigating penicillin, but it also did not seem important as he could not find a way to make it suitable to use as medicine.

Suggested change	Improved?
1. The fact that penicillin was difficult to purify, linked to the fact that it did not seem useful for treating illness, meant that there was no urgency to find a way to mass produce it.	
2. Florey and Chain decided to investigate penicillin. They found a way to produce it in slightly larger quantities and to purify it. This meant they could now carry out more experiments and they then found it was effective if injected into the bloodstream.	
3. Florey and Chain needed funding to develop the technology to mass produce penicillin but the British government did not help. However, when the USA joined the Second World War the government knew that penicillin could help to save soldiers' lives and so funding became available.	
4. The US chemical company Pfizer developed a freeze-drying technique that could be used to purify penicillin in large quantities.	

Now let's look at how to build an answer for the following question:

> Why were Florey and Chain able to mass produce penicillin by 1944? (12 marks)

You'll include the same details as in the previous question, but need to use them differently.

- Explain how each of these factors led to the mass production of penicillin.
- Explain how the factors of war and government **combined** to make it possible to mass produce penicillin by 1944 when it had not been possible in 1940.

3. Use the writing frame below to write a Level 3 answer.

Communication, such as Fleming's article on penicillin or scientists within the team sharing ideas, meant that....

....

Government action such as the US government agreeing to provide funding for the development of mass production changed the situation because....

....

War made the US government treat penicillin as a priority because....

....

The combination of war and government made it possible to mass produce penicillin by 1944 because....

....

Unit 1 is a Development Study. Questions on causation in this unit ask why change happened but also why change didn't happen (why there was continuity) or why it took so long for the situation to change. For example:

> Why were the laws against smuggling so difficult to enforce in the seventeenth and eighteenth centuries? (12 marks)
>
> The following information may help you with your answer.
>
> In 1747, customs officers seized some smuggled goods and stored them in the Customs House at Poole in Dorset. The Hawkhurst gang then attacked the Customs House during the night and got most of the goods back. They were cheered by crowds when they stopped at Fordingbridge for breakfast.

Activity

1. Study Answer A below. Underline any reasons it gives to explain why laws against smuggling were difficult to enforce.

Answer A

Smuggling was hard to detect even when it was happening because it was usually carried out in secret and at night when ships could sail close to the shore and be unloaded in the dark. There were lots of different bays and coves the smugglers could use which were too many to be watched. Also, there was no police force at this time and not enough customs officers to catch the smugglers. Lots of people got goods from the smugglers – tea, brandy, silk, tobacco and so on. These goods didn't pay tax and therefore were much cheaper than buying them in the shops which meant that people benefited from smuggling and didn't want to help the authorities. It was actually quite common for the local squire or the church minister to get things from the smugglers. However, the smugglers could also be very violent and some people were afraid of them which also meant that they would not help the authorities to catch the smugglers.

2. Read the feedback below, then complete the table on the next page to say whether each of the suggested changes would improve Answer A and, if so, why.

> This answer is clearly Level 3 because it identifies several reasons why it was so difficult to enforce the laws against smuggling but it presents them separately. It would be a top Level 3 answer if it also showed how these reasons interacted with each other, for example the fact that many respected members of society such as the minister or local squire bought goods from smugglers made other people feel there was nothing wrong with smuggling and therefore they were unlikely to help the customs officers.

Suggested change	Improved?
1. The fact that there were lots of different bays and coves that the smugglers could use, combined with the fact that there was no police force and only a limited number of customs officers, meant that there were too few people available to catch smugglers as they unloaded the smuggled goods.	
2. Usually goods would be brought from the ship to shore by rowing boat and then taken to a safe hideaway until the smuggled goods could be split into smaller amounts and sold.	
3. The local community was often involved with the smugglers. Besides buying goods from them, some people would be paid to help unload the goods, while others would store them for the smugglers. These people would side with the smugglers against the authorities.	
4. Very few people were willing to help the authorities. Some felt that the smugglers were not committing a real crime and were just helping the people to buy goods they could not normally afford; others were afraid of the large gangs who could be violent.	

3. Now let's look at how to build an answer for the following question:

Why were social crimes like smuggling and poaching so difficult to deal with in the eighteenth century? (12 marks)

To do this you'll need to explain:

○ how each factor made the situation difficult for the authorities

○ how factors **combined** to make it hard for the authorities to catch smugglers and poachers.

Use the writing frame below to write a Level 3 answer.

The nature of the crime made it difficult to detect while it was happening because smuggling and poaching were done at night and in secret so....

....

Economic conditions meant that people were sympathetic to the criminals because....

....

Social attitudes meant that people were unwilling to help the authorities because....

....

The combination of economic conditions and social attitudes made it even harder for the customs officers and gamekeepers to catch smugglers and poachers because....

....

2B The American West

In Unit 2 causation questions will often focus on people's motives for their actions, the different reasons for an event, or how events in the past affected people in different ways. They usually begin with the word 'why'. For example:

> Why did white settlers often find it difficult to understand the culture of the Plains Indians? (12 marks)
>
> You may use the following in your answer and any other information of your own.
>
> • Older Plains Indians were sometimes left behind when their tribes moved on.
> • The Plains Indians believed in Waken Tanka.
> • White settlers believed land could be bought and sold.

Below is the mark scheme for a Level 3 answer to this question. The annotations show the success criteria fulfilled by good answers.

A. Answer focuses on an explanation of why white settlers often found it difficult to understand the culture of the Plains Indians.

Level	Marks	Description of answer
3	9–12	The answer shows an understanding of the focus of the question and is able to support the factors identified with sufficient accurate and relevant detail. *E.g. clash of cultures on warfare; religious differences; social customs; nomadic lifestyle; seen as uncivilised; lacked technology.*

C. Answer gives specific and precise details.

B. Answer shows a range of reasons in the answer.

Activity

1. Read Answer A below.

a) Which TWO of the three success criteria (A, B and C) are shown in this answer? Circle your choices on the mark scheme above.

b) Use two different colours to underline where each one is met in Answer A.

Answer A

The white settlers found it difficult to understand the culture of the Plains Indians for many reasons. First, they had very different religious beliefs and so it was hard for the white settlers to understand the Plains Indians. The Indians also constantly moved. The white settlers believed in farming whereas the Indians simply didn't believe that they had the right to buy and sell land. The Plains Indians' whole existence depended on the buffalo. This meant that sometimes older members were left behind. The white settlers thought this was cruel. The Indians also used dances which white settlers did not understand. The white settlers also did not understand the Plains Indians' beliefs about warfare.

2. Now read the feedback below and rewrite Answer A to improve it.

This answer says that the key reason was that their beliefs were so different and identifies different aspects of culture that the white settlers found hard to understand. However, there are not many details about these aspects of Indian culture and therefore it is not clear why it was so difficult for white people to understand.

○ Make sure that you give a range of reasons to explain why the white settlers found it difficult to understand the culture of the Plains Indians.

○ Aim to use at least FIVE of the following terms, which will mean that you are providing specific details.

(scalping/nomadic/polygamy/Manifest Destiny/Christian/Sun Dance/Medicine Men)

....

....

....

....

Activity

3. Using the same material, write an answer to the following question on the same topic. Use a separate sheet of paper.

Why did many white settlers view the Plains Indians as savage? (12 marks)

You may use the following in your answer and any other information of your own.

• Older Plains Indians were sometimes left behind when their tribes moved on.

• The Plains Indians used the Sun Dance for help from the spirit world.

• Plains Indians often scalped dead enemies.

4. When you have written your answer, either self- or peer-assess your answer and use the check list below to show that you have fulfilled all the success criteria.

You focus on reasons why white settlers viewed the Plains Indians as savages.	
You show a range of different reasons.	
You give specific and precise details.	

In Unit 2 causation questions will often focus on people's motives for their actions, the different reasons for an event, or how events in the past affected people in different ways. They usually begin with 'why'. For example:

Why were the Nazis able to persecute the Jews in Germany in the years 1933 to 1939? (12 marks)

You may use the following in your answer and any other information of your own.

- 1935: The Nuremberg Laws were passed.
- Goebbel's Ministry of Propaganda gave daily orders to newspapers on what they could write.
- Nazi block wardens reported people who broke the law.

Below is the mark scheme for a Level 3 answer to this question. The annotations show the success criteria fulfilled by good answers.

A. Answer focuses on an explanation of why the Nazis were able to persecute the Jews in Germany in the years 1933–39.

Level	Marks	Description of answer
3	9–12	The answer shows an understanding of the focus of the question and is able to support the factors identified with sufficient accurate and relevant detail. *e.g. Nazi ideology to create a pure race; ideology of 'subhumans' and 'anti-socials'; use of SS and secret police; informers; the role of propaganda.*

C. Answer gives specific and precise details.

B. Answer shows a range of reasons in the answer.

Activity

1. Look at Answer A below. Which TWO of the three success criteria (A, B and C) are shown in this answer? Circle your choice on the mark scheme above. Use two different colours to underline where each one is met in Answer A.

Answer A

The Nazis were able to persecute the Jews for many reasons. First, the Nuremberg Laws were passed. This meant that many Jews lost their jobs and had fewer positions of power in Germany. This was a first stage in them being excluded from parts of German society. The propaganda was another reason because it influenced the way that many people thought and what they believed. In 1938 during Kristallnacht many Jewish homes, businesses and places of worship were damaged, as well as some Jews being arrested and sent to concentration camps. The use of the SS meant that many people were intimidated and were unwilling to speak out or defend the rights of German Jews. So a mixture of laws, violence and force were ways in which the Nazis were able to persecute the Jews and why this persecution got worse and worse.

2. Now read the feedback below and rewrite Answer A to improve it.

The answer identifies changes in the law, the use of violence and propaganda as key reasons why the Nazis were able to persecute Jews. However, the explanation showing how that affected people's attitudes needs to be supported with more examples. In particular, the way that propaganda built up the image of Jews as evil and 'sub-human' needs to be explained and linked to the reason why people did not care when the persecution of the Jews got worse.

○ Make sure that you give a range of reasons that explain why the Nazis were able to persecute the Jews in the years 1933 to 1939.

○ Aim to use at least FIVE of the following terms, which will mean that you are providing specific details.

(shop boycott/Aryan/marriage and sexual relations/Reich Citizenship Law/Kristallnacht/ synagogues/ Der Stürmer)

....

....

....

Activity

3. Using the same material, write an answer to the following question on the same topic. Use a separate sheet of paper.

Why did the lives of German Jews become so much more difficult in the years 1933 to 1939? (12 marks)

You may use the following in your answer and any other information of your own.

• In 1933 there was a boycott of Jewish shops.

• Goebbel's Ministry of Propaganda gave daily orders to newspapers on what they could write.

• In November 1938 many Jewish shops were attacked.

4. When you have written your answer, self- or peer-assess your answer and use the checklist below to show that you have fulfilled all three success criteria.

You focus on reasons why the lives of German Jews became more difficult.	
You show a range of different reasons.	
You give specific and precise details.	

Consequence questions

Dealing with consequences in history means thinking about the EFFECTS or RESULTS of something. You could do this by thinking about these questions:

- who was affected?

- what changed?

- how much did things change?

You should also understand that questions asking about the importance or impact of a person or event are really consequence questions. These questions are asking how the situation changed and what difference the person or event made.

How do I answer consequence questions?

We can analyse consequence in history in much the same way as we analyse causation by:

- grouping the consequences into categories such as political, social, economic or religious

- dividing them into short- and long-term consequences.

How will I be marked?

In both Unit 1 and Unit 2, questions 2, 5(a) and 6(a) are worth 9 marks. Questions 3 and 4 are worth 12 marks. However, they are all marked in the same way, using levels from Level 1 up to Level 3. A 12-mark question will usually cover a broader topic than a 9-mark question, so you will be expected to write a slightly longer answer with a wider range of details in response to a 12-mark question.

The best answers do the following things:

- Focus on EXPLANATION not description. So, rather than describing what happened afterwards, you need to show how the later situation is **linked** to, or a **consequence of**, what happened.

- Organise the answer by classifying the consequences in some way.

- Show a range of consequences. You should aim for three or four distinct points; depending on the question, this could mean three or four examples of economic consequences or one example each of the economic, social and political effects.

In Unit 1, questions on the effects or consequences of something will often ask you to link the consequences to a specific aspect of medicine. For example:

> Explain the importance of the development of the printing press in the fifteenth century and its effect on medical knowledge and understanding. (12 marks)

Activity

1. Read the question above, then look at the five points in the table below. Put a tick or cross next to each one to show whether or not it is relevant to this question about the link between the printing press and medical knowledge and understanding.

Point	Relevant?
1. During the Roman period, Galen had explained the Theory of the Four Humours and he had developed treatment based on the Theory of Opposites. His works were still being copied out and used to train doctors more than 1,000 years later.	
2. Vesalius employed an artist to produce accurate drawings of anatomy in his book *The Fabric of the Human Body*, published in 1543. This meant that doctors could gain a better understanding of the human body by studying the printed illustrations.	
3. William Harvey published his book in 1628 explaining how the heart pumped blood around the body and showing the experiments he had used in his discoveries.	
4. When something was published, many copies could be made quickly and cheaply. This meant they did not have to wait for manuscript copies to be made. Also, everyone could read an accurate copy, and there was no confusion caused by mistakes in copying.	
5. The microscope was developed during the seventeenth century.	

Hint

You can check your understanding of the question by rewriting it in different words – this question asks about the consequences of the printing press (in other words, what changes it made), but it also focuses on changes to medical knowledge and understanding during the Renaissance. It is not asking about changes in treatment.

Below is an extract from the mark scheme for a Level 3 answer to this question.

Level 3 9–12 marks	Answer shows the effects of the printing press on medical knowledge AND explains why they were important.

Read Answer A below. The answer makes a very good point about the way the printing press was an improvement over manuscripts but it needs examples to support the comment before it can be given a Level 3 mark.

Answer A

The printing press was a way of producing lots of copies of a document or picture very quickly and cheaply. Before this, every copy had to be written out by hand. This would take a long time and it could be expensive but also there was a risk of mistakes. Using the printing press meant every copy was the same and because hundreds of copies could be made very quickly, ideas could spread very quickly.

2. Use the details from points 2, 3 and 4 in the table on page 25 to rewrite and improve Answer A. Use a separate sheet of paper for this answer.

Activity

3. Practise what you have learned by planning an answer to this question:

Why was Louis Pasteur's Germ Theory in 1861 so important in improving our understanding of the causes of ill health? (12 marks)

4. Complete the 'supporting detail' sentences in the table below to help you.

Reason	Supporting detail
Before Pasteur people did not understand the causes of illness.	The most common explanations of illness were an imbalance of the humours or the belief in miasma, which meant that disease was spread by …
Pasteur's work proved that these theories were wrong.	His Germ Theory showed that …
Koch read about Pasteur's work and identified the specific microbes responsible for various diseases.	These included …
This then led on to new ways to prevent or treat different diseases.	Because they were based on an accurate understanding of the cause of disease, these new methods of prevention and treatment were more effective …

1B Crime and punishment

In Unit 1, questions on the effects or consequences of something will often ask you to link the consequences to a specific aspect of crime or punishment. For example:

Why was Elizabeth Fry important in changing attitudes towards punishment during the nineteenth century? (12 marks)

Activity

1. Read the five points in the table below. Put a tick or cross next to each one to show whether or not it is relevant to this question about the link between Elizabeth Fry and changing attitudes towards punishment.

Point	Relevant?
1. Elizabeth Fry was inspired by her Quaker religion. She visited female prisoners in Newgate Gaol, London, and took in clean straw and clothes for the women.	
2. She had the women taught how to knit and sew so that they would be less likely to go back to a life of crime when they were released. This fitted in with other ideas at the time about reforming prisoners instead of just punishing them.	
3. She wrote a book to publicise the poor conditions in prison, set up a Ladies' Association to carry out similar work in other prisons and gave evidence to parliament as part of a campaign for reform.	
4. Many of the reforms she suggested were included in Robert Peel's Gaol Act in 1823 – for example, regular visits from a chaplain to encourage the women to repent their sins and to want to live a better life.	
5. The treadmill and turning the crank were examples of hard labour carried out by prisoners later in the nineteenth century.	

Hint

You can check your understanding of the question by rewriting it in different words. This question asks about the changes in attitudes towards punishment as a result of the work of Elizabeth Fry – or, in other words, what effect did Elizabeth Fry's actions have on people's attitudes?

Below is an extract from the mark scheme for a Level 3 answer to this question.

Level 3	Answer shows the effects of the work of Elizabeth Fry AND explains why this was important.

Read Answer A. It makes a very good point about changing attitudes towards punishment, but it needs examples to support the comment before it would become a Level 3 answer.

Answer A

Elizabeth Fry's ideas were important because they fitted in with the ideas of other reformers about the value of human life and that punishment should not just be about revenge and deterrence. There was the feeling that punishment should try to reform the prisoner and rehabilitate them into society.

2. Use the details in the table on page 27 about the work done by Elizabeth Fry to re-write Answer A, turning it into a Level 3 answer. Use a separate sheet of paper for this answer.

Activity

3. Practise what you have learned by planning an answer to this question:

Why was the creation of the Bow Street Runners in the eighteenth century an important new way of dealing with crime? (12 marks)

Complete the 'supporting detail' sentences in the table below to help you.

Reason	Supporting detail
Before the Bow Street Runners there was little or no help for the victims of crime.	There were constables and watchmen but they were not very effective because …
The Bow Street Runners were set up by Henry Fielding as the first organised group to act against criminals.	They were effective because they …
When Henry Fielding died in 1754, his brother, Sir John Fielding, continued his work. He increased the number of Bow Street Runners and published the *Hue and Cry* with details of crimes and criminals.	These actions were effective because …
The Bow Street Runners set an example that was developed by Peel when he set up the Metropolitan Police.	Peel's police force was similar to the Runners because …

2B The American West

Questions dealing with consequences will often expect you to show that events changed different people's lives in different ways. For example:

> Describe the effects of the discovery of gold in California in 1848 on the settlement of the American West. (9 marks)

Here is the mark scheme for this question showing the criteria for a Level 3 answer.

Level 3	7–9 marks	Answer explains a range of effects of the discovery of gold in California in 1848 on the settlement of the American West.

There are different ways of answering this question at Level 3, provided you show at least three different effects. These effects can be either:

- effects on different groups of people OR
- different types of effects, e.g. political, social and economic effects.

Activity

First, let's look at some of the effects of the discovery of gold in California in 1848.

1. Fill in the table showing the range of ways that the discovery of gold affected the settlement of the American West.

	Example	Effect of discovery of gold
A	'the Forty-niners'	
B	Mining towns	
C	Law and order	
D	Later discoveries of gold	
E	Migration	
F	Railroads	
G	US economy	

2. Now classify these consequences in a different way. Divide them into social, economic and political effects in the table below.

Social effects	
Economic effects	
Political effects	

3. Use the space below to classify these consequences into short-term and long-term.

Short–term consequences	Long–term consequences

4. On a separate sheet of paper write a full answer to the question that shows a RANGE OF EFFECTS of the discovery of gold in California in 1848.

Activity

Look at another consequences question:

Describe the effects of the discovery of gold in the Black Hills, Dakota, in 1874 on the settlement of the American West. (9 marks)

5. Write five statements that show different consequences of this discovery of gold. Make sure you have a RANGE OF EFFECTS in your answer by covering **at least three** different groups of people or **at least three** different types of effects.

1	
2	
3	
4	
5	

2C Life in Germany

Questions dealing with consequences will often expect you to show that events changed different people's lives in different ways. For example:

> Describe the effects of hyperinflation in 1923 on Germany. (9 marks)

Here is the mark scheme for this question showing the criteria for a Level 3 answer.

Level 3	7–9 marks	Answer explains a range of effects of hyperinflation in Germany in 1923.

There are different ways of answering this question at Level 3, provided you show at least three different effects. These effects can be either:

- effects on different groups of people OR
- different types of effects, e.g. political, social and economic effects.

Activity

1. Gather information about the effects of hyperinflation on different groups of people in Germany in 1923 by filling in the table below.

	Social group	Effect of hyperinflation
A	The elderly	
B	Middle class	
C	Farmers	
D	Working class	
E	Those in debt	
F	The very rich	
G	Businessmen	

2. Now classify these consequences in a different way. Divide them into social, economic and political effects in the table below. See if you can add any other consequences.

Social effects	
Economic effects	
Political effects	

3. Use the space below to classify these consequences into short-term and long-term.

Short–term consequences	Long–term consequences

4. On a separate sheet of paper write a full answer to the question that shows a RANGE OF EFFECTS of hyperinflation.

Activity

Look at another consequences question:

Describe the effects of the Reichstag Fire in February 1933 on Hitler's rise to power.
(9 marks)

5. Write five statements that show different consequences of the Reichstag Fire. Make sure you have a RANGE OF EFFECTS in your answer by covering **at least three** different groups of people or **at least three** different types of effects.

1	
2	
3	
4	
5	

Role questions

In history we often try to see what effect an individual person or a specific factor has had on a situation. In the examination, you could be asked these kinds of questions about the role of an individual or the role of a factor:

- what role was played by …?

- how important was …?

- what impact did … have on the situation?

How do I answer role questions?

In many ways, role questions are similar to consequences questions. If the question is about the role of an individual, you would need to explain what the person did and what effect that had on the situation. If the question was about the role of a factor (for example, the government), you would need to give examples of actions carried out by the government and talk about what effect they had.

However, a role question also looks at **how** things changed, so you should explain how that person or factor interacted with other aspects of the situation. If the question asks about the impact of a person or factor, it can be helpful to compare the situation before and afterwards in order to show what difference the person or factor has made.

Remember that a person or factor could have a positive or negative influence: they could be a catalyst, speeding up the process of change, or a hindrance, slowing it down. You might feel the role of a person or factor was essential for an event to happen, or only important in combination with something else.

How will I be marked?

In both Unit 1 and Unit 2, questions 2, 5(a) and 6(a) are worth 9 marks. Questions 3 and 4 are worth 12 marks. However, they are all marked in the same way, using levels from Level 1 up to Level 3, but you will be expected to write a slightly longer answer with a wider range of details to reach the higher standard in each level.

Level 3 9–12 marks	The answer shows very clearly **how that person or factor interacted** with other aspects of the situation and **contributed to the overall result**.

Make sure your answer focuses on EXPLANATION, not description.

So, rather than describing what happened or selecting examples that involve the person or factor, you need to show how they fitted into the overall situation and contributed to the results.

Examples of questions about the role of an individual or factor that you will get in Unit 1 (Medicine or Crime) are shown on pages 34–37 and examples that you will get in Unit 2 (American West or Nazi Germany) are shown on pages 38–41.

1A Medicine and treatment

In Unit 1, examination questions can be set on certain key people. You **MUST** know about: the ideas of Galen, and the work of Andreas Vesalius, William Harvey, Edward Jenner, Louis Pasteur, Robert Koch, Florence Nightingale, Elizabeth Garrett Anderson, Alexander Fleming, and Crick and Watson. Extension Study 1 adds the influence of Hippocrates and Extension Study 2 adds Edwin Chadwick, John Snow and Anuerin Bevan.

Factors that are most often discussed in medicine are: religion, chance (luck), individuals, war, government, science, technology and social beliefs. However, there are other possibilities, such as education, medical training or communication.

Here is an example of a Unit 1 exam question that looks at the role of a factor:

Why have science and technology been so important in improving medical understanding since 1850? (12 marks)

You may use the following in your answer and any other information of your own.

- Louis Pasteur published his Germ Theory in 1861.
- X-rays were discovered in 1895.
- Crick and Watson discovered the structure of DNA in 1953.

Activity

Begin by reading Answer A.

Answer A

Science and technology have been very important in improving medical understanding since 1850. This is because Louis Pasteur published his Germ Theory in 1861 which helped people to understand about germs. He carried out experiments with liquid in two flasks. He left one flask open but bent the neck of the second flask and put water into the bend. This prevented air from reaching the liquid in the flask. This shows how science helped medicine.

An example of technology helping medicine is when Roentgen discovered X-rays. Very soon afterwards most hospitals had X-ray machines which they could use to find whether someone's bone was broken or where bullets were inside the body. We also have other technology like ultrasound scans and CAT scans.

Crick and Watson discovered DNA in 1953. This was very important because lots of conditions are the result of genetic problems.

Another example of science and technology leading to improvements in medical understanding is the production of penicillin. Fleming wrote about his discovery of penicillin in 1928 but he couldn't produce it in large quantities. Florey and Chain went to the USA to get funding to help them mass produce it.

1. Using the mark scheme extract on page 33, decide whether Answer A is a Level 3 answer and explain your reasons. Remember, the key to Level 3 is explaining how the details provided actually answer the question. In this case you need to think about whether:

- the details are examples of science and technology since 1850

- the details are used to answer this specific question, which means an explanation of how these examples improved medical understanding (notice this is NOT about treatment).

The answer is a Level .... answer because ....

....

....

2. Write a brief plan for an improved answer to this question. Use the same details but make sure you show how each example **improved** medical **understanding** (not treatment).

....

....

....

3. Analyse the following question:

> How important was the role of Elizabeth Garrett Anderson in improving the position of women within medicine in the late nineteenth century? (12 marks)

You should have spotted **the topic** (Elizabeth Garrett Anderson), **time frame** (1850–1900), **command term** (how important – what difference she made) and **focus** (improving the position of women in medicine). Now plan your answer by matching up each point with the relevant example.

1 ......   2 ......   3 ......   4 ......   5 ......

Point	Example
1. It was difficult for women to qualify and be registered as a doctor.	A. Students signed a petition to prevent her from joining their lectures and dissections; she had to pay for private sessions.
2. When Elizabeth Garrett Anderson wanted to train as a doctor she faced opposition and discrimination.	B. The Society of Apothecaries changed its regulations so that no other women could qualify in the same way.
3. She succeeded in gaining official recognition as a doctor in 1865.	C. The government passed an Act allowing women to qualify as doctors in 1876.
4. The position of women in medicine changed very little in the short term.	D. Universities and medical schools would not admit women students.
5. Her case highlighted discrimination against women but only the government could force changes.	E. Her father took the Society of Apothecaries to court to force them to register her.

1B Crime and Punishment

In Unit 1, examination questions can be set on certain key people who are named in the specification. Therefore you MUST know about: Guy Fawkes, Jonathan Wild, the Fielding brothers, Sir Robert Peel, John Howard, Elizabeth Fry and Derek Bentley.

The factors that are most often discussed in crime and punishment are: religion, individuals, economic and social conditions, government, science and technology, and social beliefs. However, there are other possibilities, such as the role of the media.

Here is an example of an exam question that asks you to consider the role of a factor.

> Why has technology been such an important factor affecting crime and policing since 1900? (12 marks)
>
> You may use the following in your answer and any other information of your own.
>
> • In 1935 the police Forensic Science Laboratory was set up.
>
> • In 1939 25 per cent of all crime involved motoring offences.
>
> • In 2001 the government set up the National High Tech Crime Squad to deal with computer crime.

Activity

Read Answer A.

Answer A

Technology has played an important role in both crime and policing since 1900. New examples of old crimes have been committed such as theft of a car or criminals being able to get away from a crime more quickly. However, there are also new types of crimes like drink-driving, not having a licence and speeding. Other new crimes have involved computers – for example, identity theft, computer hacking or sending a virus. Another example of technology is terrorism. Bombs can be set off by remote control or can use timers.

Technology has also been important for the police. Special squads have been set up to deal with car crime or with computer crime. The police also use computers to check fingerprints and keep records of individual criminals. Tracking systems linked to computers also help the police to track down criminals. The phone has been an important way for the police to communicate and also for the public to report a crime or to ask for help when they need it.

1. Using the mark scheme extract on page 33, explain whether this answer is Level 2 or Level 3. Remember, the key to Level 3 is explaining how the details provided actually answer the question. In this case you need to think about whether the details are:

  ○ examples of technology since 1900

  ○ used to answer this specific question, which means an explanation of how these examples changed crime and policing.

Answer A is a Level .... answer because ....

....

....

....

2. Write a brief plan for an improved answer to this question. Use the same details but make
sure it shows how each example of technology led to change in crime and in policing.

....

....

....

3. Analyse the following question:

How important was the role of the Fielding brothers in improving law and order in
the late eighteenth century? (12 marks)

You should have spotted **the topic** (role of the Fielding brothers), **time frame** (late
eighteenth century, i.e. **1750–1800**), **command term** (how important – what difference
they made) and **focus** (improving law and order). Plan your answer by matching up each
point with the relevant example.

1 ......   2 ......   3 ......   4 ......   5 ......

Point	Example
1. Henry Fielding was a magistrate at Bow Street who wanted to reduce crime in his area of London.	A. In 1792 London was divided into seven areas, each with three magistrates and six paid constables. In 1829, Robert Peel set up the Metropolitan Police Force.
2. In 1754 John Fielding established mounted patrols.	B. Henry printed information about crimes and criminals in the *Covent Garden Journal*.
3. Henry Fielding thought information should be shared about crime and criminals.	C. In 1763, the government paid for patrols on the main routes into London, and highway robbery soon decreased dramatically.
4. Sir John Fielding suggested that the idea of the Bow Street Runners should be extended to cover the whole of London.	D. Crime was reduced where the Bow Street horse patrols operated simply because criminals knew there was an increased risk of being caught.
5. The work of the Fieldings showed how important it was to have a well organised force available to detect and prevent crime.	E. In 1749 he set up a small group of reliable constables from the Bow Street magistrates' court to track down criminals and recover stolen property.

In Unit 2 some questions will ask you to explain the role of an individual, a group or a factor. This means looking at the impact they had on events in the past. For example:

> Describe the contribution made by women to the white settlement of the Plains. (9 marks).

Activity

Read Answer A below.

Answer A

There were lots of problems facing the early homesteaders. The weather was often severe and it was difficult to farm the land. The lack of water meant that it was difficult to farm the land. There were other hazards such as plagues of grasshoppers. Fires also damaged their farm land. But in many ways women helped the white settlement of the Plains. Women did a lot of work as they looked after the needs of the family. They collected chips for fuel (which was buffalo dung), and solved some of the problems such as making fires, cooking and heating the home. They looked after smaller animals and some of the crops. They also helped to build houses. They also looked after children. They made clothes, cooked food and made sure the family was cared for properly. Some women also helped in the white settlement of the Plains by working as teachers and there was a campaign to get female teachers. They made sure the children were cared for. Women often collected water from wells or rivers. Women were therefore important to the white settlement of the Plains.

This answer would be marked as a low Level 3.

1. Explain here why the information in the first three lines is not relevant to this question.

....

....

....

2. Underline the parts of this answer that clearly relate to the **contribution** of women to the **white settlement** of the Plains.

3. Write an improved answer to the same question, using **at least three** of the following specific details provided.

Wyoming Territory	Disease	Childbirth	Recruitment of teachers	Sod-houses

4. Here are some starters for how you can use these details to explain the contribution of women. Finish off statements A and B, then choose two more details and write a statement for each.

A. Because there were so few doctors on the Plains, women ....
....
....
....

B. Homesteaders' children needed to be educated and so women ....
....
....

C. ....
....

D. ....
....

Activity

5. Use the same information to answer a different examination question on the same topic area. Use a separate sheet of paper to write an answer to the following question:

In what ways did conditions on the Plains affect the lives of women homesteaders in the 1850s and 1860s? (9 marks)

6. Notice the dates given for this question. In the table below, put a cross by the areas **not** relevant for this particular question.

Sod-houses		Wind pumps		Building of railroads	
Disease		Education		Isolation	
Mass-produced machinery		Turkey Red wheat		Childbirth	

Here is another question on the role of a group:

Describe the part played by cattle ranchers in the Johnson County War in 1892. (9 marks)

7. On a separate sheet of paper write an answer to this question that clearly focuses on the part played by cattle ranchers in the Johnson County War and has specific supporting details.

In Unit 2 some questions ask you to explain the role of an individual, a group or a factor. This means looking at the impact they had on events in the past. For example:

> Describe the importance of the work of Goebbels as Minister of Enlightenment and Propaganda. (9 marks)

Activity

Read Answer A below.

Answer A

In the very early years of the Nazi Party, Goebbels had even been a threat to Hitler's leadership. But he then became one of Hitler's very closest supporters. Goebbels played a key role in the reorganisation of the Nazi Party after the Beer Hall Putsch. He was very good at making sure the Nazis got their message across with specific propaganda aimed at specific groups of people such as farmers, workers and women. Goebbels was very good at his job in influencing and persuading people to agree with the Nazi government. His skills were exploited by Hitler and used to maximum potential. There were mass rallies and marches which demonstrated the organisation and powerful Nazi government. People could listen to Hitler's speeches on cheapl mass-produced radios. There were new developments in technology and films such as 'The Eternal Jew' were produced that carried the Nazi message. Goebbels' work meant that Germans were influenced and Nazi ideals infiltrated the lives of ordinary people. The use of propaganda was a significant factor in preventing opposition to the Nazi government.

This answer would achieve a low Level 3 answer.

1. Explain why the information in the first four lines is not relevant to this answer.

....

....

....

2. Underline the parts of the answer that clearly relate to the **importance** of Goebbels as **Minister of Enlightenment and Propaganda**.

3. Underline the specific detail that gives an example of the importance of Goebbels' work.

4. Now write an improved answer to the same question on a separate piece of paper, using **at least three** of the specific details provided below.

Anti-Semitism	Nuremberg Rallies	Reich Chamber of Culture	Book-burnings	1936 Berlin Olympics

5. Here are some starters on how you can use these details to explain the importance of Goebbels. Finish off statements A and B, then choose two more details and write a statement for each.

A. Goebbels was important in developing ways to spread Nazi ideas such as ....

....

....

B. Goebbels wanted to make the Nazis look powerful and so ....

....

....

C. ....

....

D. ....

....

Activity

6. Use the same information to answer a different question on the same topic. Use a separate sheet of paper to write an answer to the following question.

> In what ways did the Nazi government use propaganda to control Germany in the years 1933 to 1939? (9 marks)

7. Notice the dates given for this question. Put a cross by the areas **not** relevant for this particular question.

Wall Street Crash		Munich (Beer Hall) Putsch		Nuremberg Rallies	
Berlin Olympics		*The Eternal Jew*		Images of Hitler	
Reich Chamber of Culture		Radios		Hitler Youth military units	

Here is another question on the role of an individual:

> Describe the role of Pastor Niemöller in opposing the Nazi government. (9 marks)

8. On a separate sheet of paper write an answer to this question that clearly focuses on Pastor Niemöller's role in opposing the Nazi government and has specific supporting details.

Analysis and evaluation questions

How do I answer analysis questions?

When you analyse something you break it down into key sections or points so they can each be looked at separately. You have already seen this in questions about the causes or consequences of an event, or about the role or significance of a specific person or factor. Each time you explain different reasons or effects, or different factors, you are **analysing** the situation. Both Unit 1 and Unit 2 often include questions that ask you to **analyse** change, similarity and difference, change and continuity, and importance.

Remember that you need to support your analysis with details, but make sure the details you include are used to make a point and do not just describe the situation.

How do I answer evaluation questions?

Questions that carry 16 marks, 5(b) and 6(b), might go further and ask you to **evaluate** two or more aspects. These questions can ask you to:

- decide which you think was the most important cause or consequence

- compare two different people or periods and decide which was most important

- compare two different periods and say how similar or different they were

- identify aspects of change and continuity within a period and decide which was more important.

In these questions, as well as analysing the situation, you also need to evaluate or weigh up different aspects. For example, there might be great similarity in ideas but differences in action; there might be great change for some people but more continuity for others; one factor might be important in the short term and another factor more important in the long term.

In both Unit 1 and Unit 2, questions 5(b) and 6(b) will always have three bullet points that are designed to give you some ideas about the different sorts of arguments you could use in your answer. For example, if you are being asked to compare two different people or periods, there will be at least one bullet point about each of them – this reminds you that your answer should include both of them. If you are asked about which factor or event was most important, at least one bullet point will be about the factor named in the question but at least one bullet point will be about something different, in order to remind you to think about other possibilities.

There is no 'right' answer to these questions – the best answers are any answers that go properly through the process of analysis and evaluation.

How will I be marked?

Analysis questions are usually worth 12 marks and are marked across three Levels. Evaluation questions will be worth 16 marks because you are dealing with two or more topics, analysing them in order to explain their importance or to identify change and continuity, or similarity and difference, and then making a judgement based on that analysis.

The mark scheme for evaluation questions follows the same pattern you have already seen for Levels 1, 2 and 3, but there is an additional Level 4.

Level	Marks	Descriptor
2	5–8	Answer offers relevant and accurate detail but does not show how this detail is used to answer the question.
3	9–12	Answer responds to the specific question that has been asked and analyses details to show importance, similarity or difference, change or continuity, but does not evaluate the different sides of the issue.
4	13–16	Answer responds to the thrust of the question, analysing details to show importance, similarity and difference, change and continuity, and then uses this analysis to evaluate different aspects and reach a conclusion.

In questions 5(b)/6(b), there are also additional marks for spelling, punctuation and grammar.

Spelling, punctuation and grammar

In question 5(b) and 6(b) there are additional marks for spelling, punctuation and grammar: up to 3 marks in Unit 1 and up to 4 marks in Unit 2. The table below shows how you will be marked.

Unit 1 Question 5(b)/6(b)	Unit 2 Question 5(b)/6(b)	
0 marks	0 marks	Errors severely hinder the meaning of the response or students do not spell, punctuate or use the rules of grammar within the context of the demands of the question.
Level 1: Threshold performance		Students spell, punctuate and use the rules of grammar with reasonable accuracy in the context of the demands of the question. Any errors do not hinder meaning in the response. Where required, they use a limited range of specialist terms appropriately.
1 mark	1 mark	
Level 2: Intermediate performance		Students spell, punctuate and use the rules of grammar with considerable accuracy and general control of meaning in the context of the demands of the question. Where required, they use a good range of specialist terms with facility.
2 marks	2–3 marks	
Level 3: High performance		Students spell, punctuate and use the rules of grammar with consistent accuracy and effective control of meaning in the context of the demands of the question. Where required, they use a wide range of specialist terms adeptly and with precision.
3 marks	4 marks	

Planning your answer

It is vital that your answer to an evaluation question contains an 'argument'. This does not mean insisting that your ideas are correct and other ideas are wrong or stupid. It means having a clear sense of your overall answer running through the whole essay, fitting all the jigsaw pieces of your answer together into a single picture. One section in the essay should not say that X was the most important reason something happened and then the conclusion say something different – you need to be consistent and the different parts of the essay should build up to one coherent answer.

Good answers are well structured and logical, analysing each aspect thoroughly and building up a logical argument. A good structure for your answer would be as follows.

- Introduction: state your overall argument (which was the most important factor; how similar were the two periods; how much change was there?).

- Section 1: If something is mentioned in the question (Technology was the most important reason why …), deal with that first; if nothing is mentioned, deal with the cause or factor you think is most important. If the question is about continuity or similarity, deal first with whatever is mentioned in the question, or the earlier period.

- Section 2: Deal with the alternative causes or factors, or the other side of the issue.

- Conclusion: Make your judgement, explaining your criteria clearly – how have you decided what was most important; how similar two periods were, etc.

> **Hint**
> Students who produce the best answers to evaluation questions often write a brief plan before they start writing their answer. It is a good idea to spend up to 5 minutes noting down headings for your different paragraphs.

1A Medicine and treatment

Since Unit 1 is a Development Study, change and continuity are the key themes. Therefore, except for question 1 on inference, all the questions in Unit 1 ask you to analyse change and continuity in some way. The 16-mark question comes in the Extension Studies, which cover two different periods:

- Extension Study 1 covers Medicine and public health from Roman Britain to c.1350

- Extension Study 2 covers Public health 1350 to present day.

However, the examples used below will be based on material from the specification core content, Medicine and treatment c.1350 to present day, so that they are relevant to you whichever Extension Study you have covered, and so that you can make full use of them to practise your evaluation skills and essay planning.

First let's look at this question:

> Who was more important in the development of penicillin – Fleming or Florey and Chain? (16 marks)
>
> You may use the following in your answer and any other information of your own.
>
> - 1929: Fleming published an article on penicillin.
>
> - 1940: Florey and Chain tested penicillin on mice.
>
> - 1941: Florey flew to the USA.

To answer this question properly you need to explain why Fleming was important, explain why Florey and Chain were important, and then explain your judgement about who was more important.

Activity

1. Read the following two answers A and B. In each answer, underline any explanation about importance in red and any detail in blue. Then use the mark scheme on page 43 to decide which level you think each answer should get.

Answer A

Fleming knew that many soldiers in the First World War had died of infection rather than because their wounds were so severe. After the war, Fleming carried out research to find ways of fighting the bacteria that caused infection. He was studying the enzyme lysozyme, which is found in tears, when he found that a mould had killed the bacteria he was growing for his research. Fleming studied this mould (penicillin) and found it was an antibiotic, and he successfully used it to treat an eye infection. However, it was difficult to purify and to produce in large quantities. Also, he found that it was killed by acid in the stomach so he felt that it could only be used on the skin. He could not get funding to do any more research and he did not feel it would have a big impact on medicine, so he wrote up his work in an article and went back to his original research.

During the mid-1930s Ernst Chain joined Howard Florey's research team at Oxford work on ways of fighting bacteria and, in 1939, Chain read Fleming's article. They decided to work on penicillin and tested it successfully on mice in 1940 and in 1941 on humans, but one of their patients died when supplies of penicillin ran out — they still could not produce it in large enough quantities to be effective. Florey and Chain asked British pharmaceutical companies to work with them on developing ways to purify and mass produce penicillin but they were already working at full capacity producing existing medicines; only ICI offered any help. So Florey flew to the USA to ask for help from American drug companies and the US government offered funding because the USA became involved in the Second World War and they knew how important this medicine would be in treating wounded soldiers.

By 1943 penicillin could be mass produced and was tested on soldiers in North Africa. Then in 1945 Fleming, Florey and Chain were jointly awarded the Nobel Prize for Medicine in recognition of the importance of the development of penicillin.

I think Answer A is a Level .... answer because ....

....

....

Answer B

Fleming was very important in the development of penicillin because he was the one who originally identified it as an antibiotic. He was also the person who investigated its properties and showed it could be used on humans. His article communicated his findings to the scientific community and allowed other people to continue his research when he returned to his original research.

Florey and Chain were also important because without their work, penicillin would not have become available for use on people. They overcame various obstacles to be able to purify it and mass produce it — without them, penicillin would just have remained an interesting article.

I think Answer B is a Level .... answer because ....

....

....

Read the feedback below to see if you were right.

Answer A would be awarded a mark in Level 2. It tells the story of the development of penicillin and describes the work of Fleming and of Florey and Chain, but it does not explain why they were important.

Answer B is actually far more focused on the question and does say why Fleming and Florey and Chain were important. It has the potential to be Level 3 but these comments are not supported by any details, so it would only get a Level 1 mark.

If you combined Answers A and B, you would get a Level 3 answer explaining why each of them was important in the development of penicillin. A Level 4 answer also needs to build in an evaluation of their importance. There is no 'right' answer here – any of the following arguments could make a Level 4 answer.

- Fleming was most important because if it had not been for his investigation, Florey and Chain would not have been prompted to carry out their research and develop penicillin.

- Fleming was not the most important because he researched penicillin but didn't see how it could be used in medicine and, once he had written up his findings in an article, he abandoned his research into penicillin. If Florey and Chain had not followed up on his work, penicillin would never have been developed.

- Florey and Chain were most important because they developed ways to purify penicillin and they got the funding and support from the USA to be able to mass produce it – if they hadn't done that, penicillin would never have been developed.

2. Decide which of these three arguments you agree with, then, on a separate piece of paper, write a Level 4 answer that:

- offers a judgement about who was more important

- uses phrases from Answer B to explain the importance of both Fleming and of Florey and Chain

- supports the comments with detail from Answer A.

Hint

In the examination, you would have three sides of the booklet to write your answer but you are not expected to need all that space. Try to answer this question in 1½ sides of A4 paper and remember to write a brief plan first to help you keep your answer focused.

Activity

Read this question.

How much change was there in the understanding of illness in the period c.1500–c.1900? (16 marks)

You may use the following in your answer and any other information of your own.

- 1543: Vesalius published *The Fabric of the Human Body*.

- More than 92,000 people came to be touched by King Charles II (1660–85) in an attempt to be cured of scrofula.

- 1861: Pasteur's Germ Theory.

Now read Answer C on the next page.

Answer C

In the period c.1500–c.1900 there were many changes in medicine. The work of Vesalius in getting a better understanding of human anatomy was followed up by William Harvey who published his work on the heart and the circulation of the blood in 1628. The fact that their work was published also meant that their ideas could spread quickly and by the end of the seventeenth century their work was being taught in medical schools and universities. This challenged the ideas of Galen and meant that training was no longer based on his works. Then in the eighteenth century, John Hunter dissected many bodies to get an understanding of conditions such as arthritis and how a disease progressed. Therefore by 1900 there had been huge changes in the understanding of the body and how illness affected it. However, ideas about the cause of disease remained the same for most of this period. These were that illness was caused by something supernatural (God or the movement of the planets), by miasma (that illness was caused by poisonous vapours in the air) or by an imbalance of the Four Humours.

3. Here are three sets of marks and feedback for Answer C. Decide which mark and piece of feedback is the correct one. Circle your choice.

   A. Top Level 2, 8 marks; lots of good detail about understanding of disease but little focus on change.

   B. Top Level 3, 12 marks; very good explanation of various examples of change in this period but no judgement about 'how much' change occurred.

   C. Top Level 4, 16 marks; excellent examples of change and continuity and weighs up these 2 sides of the issue in order to reach a judgement.

4. The first paragraph deals well with changes in the understanding of the body. Now, on a separate piece of paper, rewrite the second paragraph and write a conclusion in a way that would improve the answer. You should give examples of change and continuity in understanding the cause of illness by talking about how the influence of religion decreased after the seventeenth century, how miasma continued to be an accepted explanation of illness and how Pasteur's work changed people's ideas about the cause of disease. In your conclusion you should evaluate how much overall change there was in the understanding of illness.

5. On a separate sheet of paper write a plan to answer the following question.

> How similar were the ways people responded to the plague in the Middle Ages and to cholera in the nineteenth century? (16 marks)

Hint

You should include ideas about: the cause of disease; treatment; prevention and action by the authorities. Remember that if you are being asked to compare and reach a judgement on 'how similar' two things are, you have to weigh the similarities against the differences before you decide.

Below are extracts from two students' answers. Choose the one relating to your extension study and:

o underline any spelling mistakes

o circle any errors of punctuation or grammar

o rewrite the extract with accurate spelling, punctuation and grammar on a separate sheet of paper.

Extension Study 1: Medicine and public health from Roman Britain onwards

the romans made many grate advansemants in public health coz they had extreamly strong goverment that had the power and organisation for large projects like aguaducts and baths, they could rase funds in taxes and had free manpower in slaves but in middle ages it was diffrent, they had small goverments that could not raise taxs or organise large public helth projecs. romans also wanted to keep there armys fit for war so public health was important for this, this was not the case in the middle ages. romans also leart new skills and got knowlege from all over they're empire essecially the greeks but in the middle ages england were cut off and the knowlege were mostly lost, only sum remained in monasterys. but their were sum improvmants, in roman times hopsitals was just for woonded solders but in the middle ages munks and nuns ran hopsitals for evryone.

Extension Study 2: Public health c.1350 to present day

the govements roll in improving public health was more impotant during the 19th centry than the 20th centry, this is becose in 1800s not many people new the risk of deseases and becose of this only the goverment could inforce cleanliness and improvments to public health. although the goverments roll was still impotant during 20th centry it was more impotant in the 19th centry becose this was when public health reform started and without the goverments input into things like public health acts this may never of happened eg the 1st public health act was in 1848 and in 1875 they made it compulsry, without these acts and others the improvment would of been delayed so what individuals did wouldn't of mattered without goverment to inforce it.

1B Crime and punishment

Since Unit 1 is a Development Study, change and continuity are the key themes. Therefore, except for question 1 on inference, all the questions in Unit 1 ask you to analyse change and continuity in some way. The 16-mark question comes in the Extension Studies which cover two different periods:

- Extension Study 1 covers Crime and punishment from Roman Britain to c.1450

- Extension Study 2 covers Changing views of the nature of criminal activity using three case studies of witchcraft, conscientious objectors and domestic violence.

However, the examples used here will be based on material from the specification core context, Crime and punishment c.1450 to present day, so that they are relevant to you whichever Extension Study you have covered, and so that you can make full use of them to practise your evaluation skills and essay planning.

Who was more important in the reform of prisons – John Howard or Elizabeth Fry? (16 marks)

You may use the following in your answer and any other information of your own.

- 1777: John Howard published a report on the state of prisons in England and Wales.

- 1785: a new prison was built at Gloucester that used many of Howard's ideas.

- 1813: Fry visited the women's section of the prison at Newgate, London.

To answer this question properly you need to explain why John Howard was important, explain why Elizabeth Fry was important, and then explain your judgement about who was more important.

Activity

1. Read the following two answers A and B. In each case, underline any explanation about importance in red and any detail in blue. Then use the mark scheme on page 43 to decide which level you think each answer should get.

Answer A

John Howard became Sheriff of Bedfordshire in 1773 and inspected the prisons in his county. He found that they were dirty and crowded with many abuses of the prisoners. Prisoners had to pay for their food and accommodation which meant that the rich could get private rooms and good food while the poor were all in one big room and didn't even get clean straw to lie in. Female prisoners were often raped by the guards, and young criminals or people in for petty crimes mixed with older criminals, often learning new methods of committing crimes. Howard then carried out a systematic survey of all the prisons in England and Wales, measuring the space, checking the food and recording the fees system. Howard recommended that the gaolers should be paid, which would prevent them charging the prisoners for necessities, that prisoners should be separated by sex and according to their crimes, and that a doctor and a chaplain should visit regularly. He wanted prisoners to be reformed through education, religion and work so they could learn a trade and support themselves when they came out of prison, instead of going back to crime.

Elizabeth Fry was shocked to find that 300 women prisoners were crowded into three rooms at Newgate prison and that many of them were ill and cold because they could not afford to pay for medical treatment or bedding. She took in clean straw and clothes for the women, persuaded the prison authorities to set up a school for the children who were in prison and suggested changes such as female prison guards and the prisoners being taught a trade. She set up a chapel in the prison and introduced sewing as a compulsory activity for the women. Fry was invited to give evidence to parliament in 1818 but changes were not made until Peel's Gaol Act in 1823. She also toured prisons in England and Scotland and set up Ladies' Associations to visit prisoners and help improve conditions in other prisons.

As prison began to be used as a punishment, the number of prisoners increased and by 1818 there were 107,000 prisoners. When Sir George Paul, the High Sheriff of Gloucestershire, had a new prison built in 1785, it was based on Howard's ideas, as were several other new prisons in the nineteenth century, such as Pentonville (built in 1842), Dartmoor (1850) and Brixton (1853). In the mid-nineteenth century, two prison systems developed — the separate system, based on the idea of work and religion being used to reform prisoners, and the silent system, based on hard labour, punishment and deterrence.

I think Answer A is a Level .... answer because ....

....

....

Answer B
John Howard was very important because he was a High Sheriff and therefore a respected person, in a position of authority. His book publicised his findings and drew widespread attention to the abuses in the system for the first time. However, new prisons based on his ideas were expensive to build and to run. Elizabeth Fry was important because she showed that 30 years after Howard's report, conditions were still appalling in many prisons. Giving evidence to parliament was significant because parliament is the only organisation which can actually change the laws and enforce changes across the whole country. Her Ladies' Associations helped to improve conditions at other prisons and her work was admired by Queen Victoria.

I think Answer B is a Level .... answer because ....

....

....

Now read the feedback below to see if you were right.

Answer A describes the conditions in prison, describes the work of John Howard and Elizabeth Fry and describes some changes that were made to the prison system; it would be awarded a mark in Level 2.

Answer B is actually far more focused on why Howard and Fry were important. It has the potential to be Level 3, but the comments are not supported by any details so it would get a Level 1 mark.

If you combined Answers A and B, you would get a Level 3 answer explaining why each of them was important in prison reform. A Level 4 answer needs to build in an evaluation of their importance. There is no 'right' answer here – any of the following arguments could make a Level 4 answer.

○ Howard was more important because he raised awareness of the problem and based his report on detailed evidence from all the prisons in England and Wales, which meant it could not be ignored or dismissed as something that just happened in a few prisons.

○ Howard was not more important because there had been so little progress by the time Fry visited Newgate that his ideas were clearly not being acted on.

○ Fry was more important because she brought in specific reforms at Newgate and then set up Ladies' Associations to spread these reforms to other prisons.

2. Decide which of these arguments you agree with, then, on a separate piece of paper, write a Level 4 answer which:

○ offers a judgement about who was more important

○ uses phrases from Answer B to explain the importance of both Howard and Fry

○ supports the comments with detail from Answer A.

Read the following question and then Answer C on the next page.

How much change was there in the methods used to catch criminals in the period c.1500–c.1900? (16 marks)

You may use the following in your answer and any other information of your own.

• In the sixteenth century towns and villages relied on unpaid constables and the 'hue and cry' to catch criminals.

• 1749: Bow Street Runners founded.

• 1878: Criminal Investigations Department set up.

Answer C

In the period c.1500–c.1900 there were many changes in the methods of law enforcement. During the sixteenth century each village had a constable, although he was not usually very efficient because he was appointed for only a year and was not paid. The 'hue and cry' was a system where anyone who witnessed a crime had to chase the criminal, shouting to draw attention to him, but many people ignored the shouts. In the reign of Charles II regulations were drawn up about the duties of nightwatchmen but these men were often old and unlikely to chase after criminals. So the work of the Fielding brothers, who set up the Bow Street Runners and horse patrols in London during the eighteenth century, was a major change. For the first time there was a trained and paid group of men who were expected to track down and catch criminals. This idea was further developed by Robert Peel in 1829 when he set up the Metropolitan Police Force and in 1856 it became compulsory for every area of the country to have a professional police force. By 1900, the police had developed specialised groups such as the CID, to solve crimes using new technology such as photographs and fingerprints.

However, the changes only really began in 1749 and most of them happened after 1829. For most of this period, there was no real system of catching criminals, and it was not until 1856 that changes happened which affected the whole country.

3. Here are three sets of marks and feedback for Answer C. Decide which mark and pice of feedback is the correct one. Circle your choice.

   A. Top Level 2, 8 marks; lots of good detail about different aspects of law enforcement but little focus on change.

   B. Top Level 3, 12 marks; very good explanation of various examples of change in this period but no judgement about 'how much' change occurred.

   C. Top Level 4, 16 marks; excellent examples of change and continuity and weighs up these 2 sides of the issue in order to reach a judgement.

4. The first paragraph deals well with changes in ways to catch criminals. Now, on a separate piece of paper, rewrite the second paragraph and write a conclusion in a way that would improve the answer. You should give examples of continuity in the methods used to catch criminals by talking about the lack of a professional body and the emphasis on the community for most of the period. In your conclusion you should evaluate how much overall change there was in the methods used to catch criminals.

5. On a separate sheet of paper write a plan for an answer to the following question.

> How similar were social crimes in the eighteenth century, such as smuggling and poaching, and the social crimes in the twentieth century such as smuggling, and tax evasion? (16 marks)

Hint

Make sure you find examples of both similarity and difference in the nature of the crimes, the way they were carried out and people's reactions to them. Then weigh up whether the crimes were basically the same or very different

Below are extracts from two students' answers. Choose the one relating to your extension study and:

○ underline any spelling mistakes

○ circle any errors of punctuation or grammar

○ rewrite the extract with accurate spelling, punctuation and grammar on a separate sheet of paper.

Extension Study 1: Crime and punishment from Roman Britain onwards

law and order in england under the roman's and norman's was quiet similar cos many elements of the roman system remained the same during the norman rein such as wipping execution and fines as punishments as well as trials crimes and policing. the king or emperer in roman and norman times had absulute power and controlled everything and to be called a trator resulted in execution in both periods. there was no police forse in either periods but their were similar groups like vigils, urban cohortes and praitorian gard in roman times who did jobs like stopping riots and putting out fires and garding the emperer, and the norman's had hue and cry which meant that if you saw a crime comitted you had to announce it and the blood fued which meant that if someone killed your relative you had the right to kill them.

Extension Study 2: Changing views of the nature of criminal activity c.1450 to present day

concientous objecters were new criminels in wwl when conscription was brought in and those refusing to fight had to have a good reason to excuse them from fighting, pasifism was common with quakers and ecomonic and political reasons was also common but morel reasons was too. in wwl concientous objecters were treated as crimes if they wasn't excused from fighting, the public would give them white feathers simbolising that there cowards and the authorities sent them to prison. in 1916 many absolutists were sent to dartmor prison and some were sent to military prison's in france. some died in prison or afterwoods.

2B The American West

The question below is asking you to look at the changes to the lives of cowboys in the years 1865–80. You need to think about what was happening to make changes to cowboys' lives during this period.

Why did the lives of cowboys change in the period 1865–80? (12 marks) You may use the following in your answer and any other information of your own.

- 1866: about 260,000 cattle were driven from Texas to the rail-head at Sedalia.

- In 1870 Charles Goodnight set up a ranch on the Great Plains.

- In 1880 36,600 tonnes of barbed wire were made and sold.

Hint

Questions 3, 4, 5(b) and 6(b) will always have some bullet points to help you with your answer. You do not have to use these at all, but they are there to help give you some ideas that you may find useful for your answer.

Activity

Look at Answer A, which shows a good Level 3 answer.

1. Use one colour to underline where the answer EXPLAINS changes to cowboys' lives.

2. Use a separate colour to underline key specific and accurate information.

Answer A

The lives of cowboys changed dramatically from 1865–1880. There were a number of factors which brought this about. In 1866 the first cattle trail was set up and approximately 260,000 cattle were driven from Texas to the rail-head at Sedalia. This was because after the American Civil War in 1865, cattle ranchers came back from the war to Texas to find that their cattle livestock had grown considerably to 5 million. There was a low demand for beef in Texas but there was a high demand in the northern states and therefore profit to be made. Therefore ranchers set off on the long drive and this changed their lives.

Furthermore, John Iliff realised that Texas Longhorns could survive the Plains' severe climate and so set up a ranch on the Great Plains. As a result more ranchers set up on the Plains and so cowboys began to move from Texas.

Also, Glidden patented barbed wire and this was a major reason for the end of the open range. Cowboys had to adapt to this and this changed their lives. Lastly, 1869 marked the completion of the first trans-continental railroad connecting east and west. Consequently, cowboys' lives were changed as they could now take their cattle to the railroads and they could be transported efficiently to states far away. This saved the cowboys a lot of time and effort and reduced their work.

Activity

Here is another question that focuses on change:

> What changes did the coming of railroads make to the development of the Great Plains? (12 marks)
>
> • 1869: The opening of the first trans–continental railroad.
> • Abilene was built on the Kansas–Pacific railroad.
> • Farming equipment was made in the eastern states.

Read through Answer B below.

Answer B

Before the coming of the railroads it was very difficult to cross the Great Plains. People had made very difficult and dangerous journeys by wagon train. The wagon trains could be made up of around 20 wagons. Sometimes this ended in disaster, like the Donner Party which had left in 1846. The wagon train got trapped in the severe weather and some of them only survived by being cannibals. By 1860 the US government were keen to help develop railroads for a number of reasons. As well as the idea of 'Manifest Destiny' the railroads would make it easier to solve problems of law and order as well as helping develop America's economy with the Far East. New cities grew on the western coast such as San Francisco. The railroads provided lots of jobs. New developments in machinery (such as wind pumps and barbed wire) which were made in the east could now be transported west. Homesteaders became much less isolated. Goods could be delivered to the west. The cattle industry also grew. The development of the railroads also had effects on the lives of the Plains Indians. It was much harder for the Plains Indians to hunt buffalo.

3. Underline the examples of specific and accurate information in this answer.

4. Cross out the parts of the answer which are irrelevant for this question.

5. Using a separate sheet of paper improve the answer by clearly explaining the changes brought by the coming of the railroads to the development of the Plains.

Here is an example of the type of question 5(b) or 6(b) you will in get in the exam:

Technology was the most important factor in solving the problems faced by homesteaders in the 1870s and 1880s. Do you agree? Explain your answer. (16 marks)

You may use the following in your answer and any other information of your own.

- 1869: The first railroad crossed the Great Plains.

- 1873: The US government passed the Timber and Culture Act.

- 1880s: Homesteaders started growing Turkey Red wheat.

Hint
The first bullet point gives you an idea for the argument in the question. The other two bullet points might give you other arguments that you can use.

6. In Answer C below place the corresponding letter for each of the feedback below in the space where you think they should go.

A. Level 2 This is a description of problems facing homesteaders.	**B. Level 4** This shows a clear analysis of the statement in the question.	**C.** This is not relevant to this particular question – this is not related to the lives of homesteaders in the 1870s and 1880s.
D. Level 3 Here the student is explaining how technology helped the homesteaders.	**E. Level 4** Here the student is weighing up and evaluating the statement.	**F. Level 4** Here the student reaches a judgement on the statement and explains why.

Answer C

The homesteaders had many problems in the 1870s and 1880s. The land on the Plains was very dry in the summer, it had never been farmed before and the winters were severe. The Plains are a vast area and they lived very isolated lives. Many lived in sod houses – but it was very hard to keep these clean and hard to prevent the spreading of disease. There were also problems of plagues of locusts and grasshoppers. [.......] In 1862 the government passed the 1862 Homestead Act which allowed white settlers to claim some land – and they first started to become known as homesteaders. [.......]

Technology played a vital role in improving the homesteaders' lives. First of all the coming of the railroads meant that during the 1870s and 1880s their lives became much less isolated. It also meant that manufactured goods and agricultural machinery (such as reapers and threshers) from the east could easily be transported and were cheaper for the homesteaders to buy. [.......] Technology also saw the invention of barbed wire in 1874 and this meant that homesteaders could farm without the danger of cattle damaging their land. This meant that the homesteaders could farm more land easily without needing extra men. Other technology that helped homesteaders' farming problems was the availability of wind pumps by the 1880s.

So technology played a major part in improving homesteaders' lives in the 1870s and 1880s. [.......] But there were other factors that improved the lives of homesteaders. The government played a role by making land more affordable with the 1873 Timber and Culture Act. As well as this, the arrival of "Turkey Red" was due to the arrival of Russian migrants and this proved to be an effective crop.

On the whole technology helped to solve a significant number of problems for the homesteaders — but the government and new crops also played a role. [.......] Although these factors all solved many of the problems facing homesteaders they would never be able to solve some of the problems they faced, such as very hot summers and very dry winters. [.......]

Activity

Now let's look at another evaluation question.

The Battle of the Little Big Horn was a victory for the Plains Indians. Do you agree? Explain your answer. (16 marks)

You may use the following in your answer and any other information of your own.

• General Custer and more than 250 of his army officers were killed.

• Custer was seen as a hero by the American public.

• 1877: Crazy Horse was captured and later killed by the US Army.

7. Use two colours and underline clearly where you think Answer D is a Level 3 answer and where you think it becomes a Level 4 answer.

Answer D

The Battle of Little Big Horn can be seen both as a victory for the Plains Indians but also as a defeat. First, when the whites found gold in the Black Hills they broke the 1868 Fort Laramie Treaty which stated the whites would not go into what was sacred land for the Indians. This angered the Indians and they killed nearly 100 whites at Rosebud river. The army was sent to protect the whites but they foolishly split up. When Custer and his army located the Indians he charged and his men were slaughtered. This is significant as it shows Custer's mistakes and the disorganisation of his army. The battle united the Indians and they had better weaponry than the US army.

It can also be seen as a defeat for the Indians. After the battle the US government was outraged. The battle triggered the US government to order the Indians onto reservations. This made the US army determined to capture Crazy Horse. Without their chiefs the Indians were not as well organised. Also Little Big Horn was a defeat for the Indians in that they were outnumbered by the whites and so could easily be forced onto reservations.

Therefore in conclusion many could agree or disagree with the statement. The Indians won the battle in the very short term, but in the very long term it meant that the US army and US government were even more determined to regain control.

Activity

Below is a student answer with a number of spelling, punctuation and grammar errors. Read the answer and then:

○ underline any spelling mistakes

○ circle any errors of punctuation or grammar

○ rewrite the extract with accurate spelling, punctuation and grammar on a separate sheet of paper.

the coming of the railrode in 1865–85 was important to the growth of cattel ranshing, it meant more faster and easier access to heavily populated easten states, this is significant becose the beef could be sold where it is more in demand. also another reason of the growth of cattel ranshing was the cattel trails north. charles goodnight came back from the civil war to find his 180 cows had turned into 5000 longhorn's, charles goodnight and his assitant oliver loving decided to move the longhorn's north, this is important becose as the cattel trail north was successful other ranshs were influenced to do the same, the cattel ranshs made profit by going north. another reason was the cow towns, joseph mccoy was the 1st person to set up a cow town abilene, the development of the cow town meant cowboy's could have somewhere to stay while on cattel trails, the town also provided servises, socailising and cattel auctions. this is important becose it is creating more money for the cattel industry making it more powerful.

The question below is asking you to look at the changes to the lives of women in the years 1933 to 1939. You need to think about what was happening to make changes to women's lives during this period.

In what ways did the lives of women in Nazi Germany change in the years 1933 to 1939? (12 marks)

You may use the following in your answer and any other information of your own.

- 1933: Law for the Encouragement of Marriage.
- Education for girls stressed Domestic Science.
- 1936: There was a shortage of workers in Germany.

Hint

Questions 3, 4, 5(b) and 6(b) will always have some bullet points to help you with your answer. You do not have to use these at all – but they are there to help give you some ideas that you may find useful for your answer.

Activity

Look at Answer A below. It is a good Level 3 answer.

1. Use one colour to underline where the answer EXPLAINS changes to women's lives.

2. Use a separate colour to underline key specific and accurate information.

Answer A

The Nazis had very clear ideas about the roles of women in society and passed laws to put these into practice. One such law was the Encouragement of Marriage in 1933. This made it clear that women were desired by the Nazi government to be married and to look after children. The government gave a loan of 1,000 marks to every couple that got married. This shows how much Hitler was ready to ensure women got married. The Nazi government also used propaganda to demonstrate what they believed were typical female characteristics. The 3Ks were publicised ('cooking, children and church'), which again emphasised what was expected of women. It was made clear through propaganda posters that women were not supposed to wear short skirts or use make-up. They made it clear what the Nazis' beliefs were about pure Aryan women. The Nazis also introduced special medals for the number of children women had (bronze for four children, silver for six and gold for eight). This shows us the expectations of women in Nazi Germany and their duties for the future of the "1000 year Reich." Many professional women lost their jobs as teachers and working for the government. Girls were also taught their future roles as mothers in school with Domestic Science lessons which stressed their importance for the future of Germany.

However in 1936 more women were needed for work. The Nazis were not totally successful in removing women from the workplace. More women were needed because of the shortage of workers – especially in factories making weapons. This meant that the government had to change the marriage loans scheme so that women could also work.

Activity

Here is another exam question which focuses on change:

In what ways did the Nazis' treatment of the Jews change in the years 1938–1945? (12 marks)

- November 1938: German Jews and property were attacked during Kristallnacht (Night of the Broken Glass).
- 1939: The beginning of the Second World War.
- 1942: The use of Zyklon B gas at Auschwitz.

Read Answer B below.

Answer B

Soon after Hitler became chancellor of Germany the Nazis ordered the one-day boycott of Jewish shops. They had signs outside saying that anybody using these shops were traitors to Germany. Following this the Nuremberg Laws were passed and this made sexual relations and marriage between 'pure' Germans and Jews illegal. The Nazis' treatment of the Jews changed drastically in the years 1938 to 1945 and became much more extreme. After the murder of Von Rath, Kristallnacht occurred and many German Jews were attacked and their properties, businesses and places of worship were destroyed. The Jews were even ordered to pay compensation for the attacks on their property. A year later the Second World War broke out. The Nazis believed in the idea of lebensraum which meant expanding towards the east. The Nazis used their special Einsatzgruppen forces who killed many Jews in Eastern Europe. Also many Jews were forced to live in ghettos such as the one in Warsaw. Here many died of disease (such as typhus) and lack of food. In January 1942 leading Nazis met at Wannsee where the planning of the 'Final Solution' was discussed. Death camps were purposefully planned. Over the next two years train loads of Jews from many European countries were sent to these camps. On arrival at the camps, SS officers divided the prisoners into those for immediate death and the others were used for slave labour. In the very last stages of the Second World War, some prisoners died on the 'death marches'. By the end of the Second World War it is estimated that 6 million European Jews had been killed by the Nazis.

3. Underline the examples of specific and accurate information in this answer.

4. Cross out the parts of the answer which are irrelevant for this question.

5. Using a separate sheet of paper write an improved version of Answer B by clearly explaining changes in the Nazis' treatment of the Jews in the years 1938–1945.

Activity

Here is an example of the type of question 5(b) or 6(b) you will in get in the exam.

'The main role of education in Nazi Germany was to prepare boys and girls for different roles.' Do you agree? Explain your answer. (16 marks)

• Girls studied Domestic Science.

• Boxing was compulsory in school for boys.

• All pupils had lessons in Race Studies.

Hint
The first two bullet points agree with the statement in the question. The final bullet point might give you another argument you can use.

6. In Answer C below place the corresponding letter for each piece of feedback in the space where you think it should go.

A. Level 2	B. Level 4	C. This is not relevant to
This is description of Nazi education policies.	This shows a clear analysis of the statement in the question.	this particular question – this is not related to education but youth.
D. Level 3	E. Level 4	F. Level 4
Here the student is explaining Nazi education policies.	Here the student is weighing up and evaluating the statement.	Here the student reaches a judgement on the statement and explains why.

Answer C

I partly agree with the statement that the main role of education in Nazi Germany was to prepare boys and girls for different roles. There were different timetables for boys and girls. For example, boys were taught more PE and girls had more lessons in subjects such as Domestic Science. This was because the Nazis wanted the girls to grow up and be fit and healthy and so have healthy children [........]. The boys were being prepared for their future roles in the armed forces. There were even special Adolf Hitler Schools which were to prepare future Nazi leaders. So the Nazis were using education to prepare boys and girls for their future roles. This happened outside of schools too and in the Hitler Youth and the League of German Maidens. In the youth groups boys again were taught more skills to prepare them as future soldiers and the girls as future mothers. [........] Later on there would be marriage loans so that more women would give up their work and also they would get medals for the number of children they had. Therefore to some extent I agree with the statement. [........]

However both boys and girls were taught Race Studies. This was so that the Nazis could spread their anti-Semitic message. This included learning things such as what Jews looked like and blaming them for Germany's problems. As well as Race Studies, both boys and girls would learn Nazi ideas in other subjects such as Maths, German and History. In these lessons they would learn about how many bombs were needed for bombing other countries, Germany's need for expansion into the east and the unfairness of the Treaty of Versailles. [........]

Therefore, in conclusion, I partly agree with the statement that education was mainly to prepare boys and girls for different roles. This was clearly a main aim of Nazis. But in some ways they did not want to educate people, but to train them into their way of thinking. [........] Therefore both boys and girls learnt in lessons about other Nazi ideas such as anti-Semitism. Education was both to prepare boys and girls for different but equally important roles – [........] but was also to brainwash, indoctrinate and make as many Germans as possible into loyal Nazis.

Now let's look at another evaluation question:

'The Wall Street Crash was the most important reason for the increase in support for the Nazis in the years 1928–1932.' Do you agree? Explain your answer. (16 marks)

- 1928: The Nazis had less than 3 per cent of the vote.

- 1932: A Nazi election poster had the caption 'Hitler – Our Last Hope!'

- 1932: Unemployment in Germany reached 6 million.

7. Use two colours and underline clearly where you think Answer D is a Level 3 answer and where it becomes a Level 4 answer.

Answer D

Yes, I agree that the Wall Street Crash was the most important reason for the increase in support for the Nazis in the years 1928–1932. This is because until the Wall Street Crash, the Weimar Republic was on the road to recovery. The Wall Street Crash was when the Stock Exchange suddenly collapsed in New York. This meant that the USA could no longer lend Germany money but also ordered all the loans to Germany to be paid back immediately. This meant that businesses went bankrupt and so unemployment started rising in Germany. Many Germans began turning to extremist political parties and one of these was the Nazi Party. By 1932 unemployment reached 6 million. Many Germans were living in desperate poverty and were even using soup kitchens in major cities such as Berlin. This is when the Nazis gained much more support. Nazi propaganda posters were used such as 'Hitler – Our Last Hope'. This was what many Germans were looking for – someone they thought could make Germany powerful again. He promised things such as getting rid of the Treaty of Versailles and getting Germany out of depression. The Wall Street Crash therefore created the crisis which made much of this possible. Many of the working class wanted jobs and many of Germany's middle class were scared of inflation again and they had suffered when many had lost their savings and pensions in 1923.

Of course, other factors helped the rise in support for the Nazis. The Nazi Party themselves used clever propaganda to get as much support as possible. Hitler had the support of business and newspapers as well and eventually Hindenburg offered him the job of chancellor. But without the Wall Street Crash, Germany would have carried on recovering as it had under Stresemann and Hitler would not have been able to use the crisis. Therefore the Wall Street Crash was the main and most important factor in Hitler's rise to power.

Activity

Below is a student answer with a number of spelling, punctuation and grammar errors. Read the answer and then:

- underline any spelling mistakes
- circle any errors of punctuation or grammar
- rewrite the extract with accurate spelling, punctuation and grammar on a separate sheet of paper.

the wall st crash was the most important reason for the incraese in support for the nazi's in 1928–32 as germany was too reliant on america and the nazi's need kaos to help them get more votes. in 1932 umenployment rose to 6m people becose of the wall st crash as employer's didn't have that much money to give out, the nazi's also used propoganda like radio broadcasts newspapers and posters to publish the fact that germany is becoming kaotic and hilter has the answer. before the wall st crash happened the nazi's only had less than 3% of votes which wasn't alot becose germany wasn't in an awful state, it still had a chance to be great again. after the crash umenployment had rose to 6m german people and hilter and the nazi's could use this to there advantage and they promised that when the nazi's are in power people will have jobs again, as a result of the promises they made the nazi's got more votes. the nazi's could also advetise that hilter was they're best hope through propoganda, cleverly using the kaos from the wall st crash. when hilter did his speech's he only spoke about what people wanted to hear like an end to inflation and end to umenployment. the nazi's needed something really bad like the wall st crash to happen to be able to get into power.

Unit 3 Introduction

What is Unit 3 about?

Unit 3 is a source enquiry unit. There are four options in this unit and you will be studying one of them. This book covers the following two options. Highlight the option you have studied:

- Option 3A: The transformation of surgery c.1845–c.1918

- Option 3B: Protest, law and order in the twentieth century

What do I need to know?

You have to answer five questions, each testing different source skills, including:

- making supported inferences (see pages 73–78)

- explaining the message or purpose of a source (see pages 73–78)

- cross-referencing three sources (see pages 79–83)

- evaluating the utility of two sources (see pages 84–89)

- using sources and own knowledge to reach a judgement (see pages 90–97)

The knowledge that you have about the topic is called contextual knowledge and you must make use of it in question 5.

What will the exam paper be like?

You have 75 minutes to answer this exam paper. It is worth 53 marks. You will be given a Source Booklet with six to eight sources (labelled A–H) on a topic within your option. They will be a mixture of written sources and illustrations. You have to answer five questions on these sources.

- Question 1 is an inference question on Source A and is worth 6 marks.

- Question 2 is a source analysis question on Source B; it is focused on portrayal and is worth 8 marks.

- Question 3 is a cross-referencing/comparison question and is worth 10 marks; it will usually involve at least one source you have already used and at least one new one, for example, Sources B, C and D.

- Question 4 will ask you to compare the utility or value of two sources and is worth 10 marks.

- Question 5 will give you an issue or comment ('hypothesis') and ask you to use three sources and your contextual knowledge to reach a judgement. It is worth 16 marks, plus up to 3 additional marks for spelling, punctuation and grammar.

The guidance on the next two pages gives you an overview of the key source skills you'll need to use in the source paper. You will then look at each question type in turn to help you to practise those skills on sources which are suitable for the option you are studying.

You will need to make use of a variety of skills when you answer source questions. These include annotating sources, making use of the contents of sources and of your contextual knowledge and understanding, as well as being able to apply the criteria of nature, origins and purpose of sources. These are shown in the following examples.

Annotating sources
First of all read the question before you look at the relevant source or sources. This will ensure that you make full use of the source. You may find it useful to annotate the sources as you read them, either by highlighting or underlining the key information. Remember to also make use of the information given above the source which is known as the provenance – that is, who produced the source and when, and what type of source it is. In a written source, you should highlight the key words or phrases in the source itself. In illustrations, you should highlight the key features and people shown. This will help you to work out what the source is suggesting.

Contextual knowledge
This means the knowledge that you have about a topic or event. This knowledge will help you with your source skills because:

- it will ensure that you understand what the source is suggesting

- it will enable you to make judgements about the source itself – how accurate it is, how well it has covered the event.

For example, using Source A opposite, it would be helpful to know that the poster was produced during the Second World War at a time when Britain was alone in facing Germany and Italy. Winston Churchill was popular with most British people because of his determination not to surrender.

Contextual knowledge is not required at all in questions 1–4, so there is no need to worry if you have not studied a particular topic or event mentioned in the sources. Contextual knowledge is **only** needed in question 5 where it can help you to explain something mentioned in the sources in more detail, or to bring in a new idea. However, if you have a good understanding of the key issues, you only need a few details from your own knowledge to support your explanation.

Contents
This is the information which the source gives you about an event or person. You will need to identify information such as dates and actual events as well as opinions and points of view. For example, in Source A you can see:

- Winston Churchill, the prime minister, in the foreground

- a catchy slogan

- tanks and fighter planes in the background.

The nature, origins and purpose of sources

This approach helps you to make use of the provenance of the source and why the source was produced.

Source A: A poster issued by the British government in late 1940

Nature

This means the type of source. Is it a poster, photograph, cartoon, speech, diary, letter?

This is a poster. Posters are usually produced for propaganda purposes to persuade people to think or act in a certain way.

Origins

This means when the source was produced and by whom.

This was produced by the British government in late 1940.

Purpose

This means why the source was produced. What is it trying to make you do? Who is it trying to make you support?

This is an example of a propaganda poster which is trying to get support for the Prime Minister and the war effort, and to keep up the morale of the British people.

Source A: The Old Operating Theatre at St Thomas's Hospital, London. This room was bricked up in the mid-nineteenth century but rediscovered in 1956 and restored to show how it would have appeared.

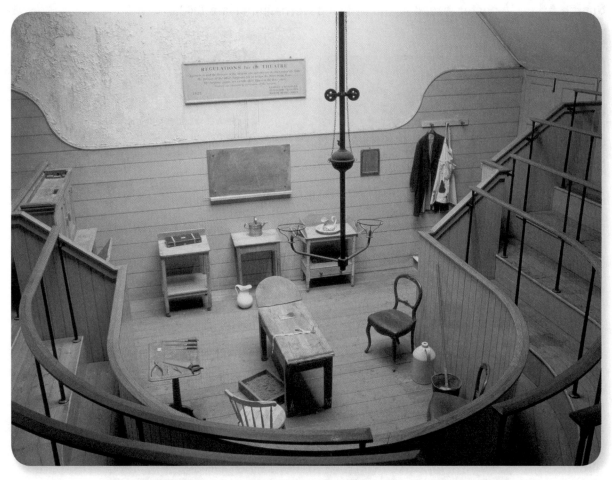

Source B: From an account by the Professor of Chemistry at Edinburgh University, describing Simpson's attempts to find a better anaesthetic than ether.

On one occasion he came into my laboratory to ask whether I had any new substance likely to produce anaesthesia. My assistant had just prepared a liquid which I thought worthy of experiment. Simpson, who was brave to the point of rashness in his experiments, wished to try it upon himself. This I absolutely refused to allow, and declined to give him any of the liquid unless he promised me first to try its effect on rabbits. Two rabbits were brought, and under the vapour quickly passed into anaesthesia, coming out of it in due course. Next day, Simpson proposed to experiment upon himself and his assistant with this liquid but the assistant suggested that they should first see how the rabbits had fared. They were both found to be dead.

Source C: From a letter by Dr Liston, after he had used ether on patients during two operations.

I tried the ether inhalation today in a case of amputation of the thigh, and in another on the great toe-nail, which is one of the most painful operations in surgery. In both operations I had the most perfect and satisfactory results. It is a very great thing to be able to destroy pain to such an extent, and without, apparently, any bad result. It is a fine thing for operating surgeons.

continued overleaf

Source D: From a report of a speech by Professor Syme, a leading surgeon, to the Medical Society of Edinburgh in 1849. He is speaking here about the use of chloroform in surgery.

After it was proposed by Dr. Simpson, Syme used it in the first operation he had to perform in the hospital and ever since then he had continued to use it. He desired to state to the Society that he believed anaesthesia not only saved patients operated on from pain, but also from shock, and all its effects. When Dr. Simpson first stated this as his opinion, Mr Syme had strongly opposed it but now he was convinced that Dr Simpson was right.

Source E: From a report in *The Lancet*, a medical journal, published on 22 December 1849.

An inquest* was held at Shrewsbury upon the body of a poor Welsh girl. It appeared that it was necessary for her to undergo a very painful operation, the removal of the eyeball. The surgeon administered about one-third of the quantity of chloroform he has given to other patients. It had, however, such an effect upon her that she was seized with apoplexy**. The jury returned a verdict of 'Died by apoplexy, caused by inhaling chloroform'.

  * An inquest is an investigation into why someone died

  ** Apoplexy was often used to describe a stroke

Source F: An illustration showing the unveiling of a statue of Simpson in Edinburgh, 1877.

Source A: A leaflet describing the force-feeding of suffragettes in a Liverpool prison in December, 1909.

At night she was kept in irons. Next day she was thrown down with her face upon the floor. Face downwards, her arms and legs were dragged up until she was lifted from the ground. Her hair was seized by another wardress. In this way she was marched up the steps her head bumping on the stone stairs. In the room the operation of forcible feeding was performed - causing a terrible state of physical and mental distress. She was handcuffed again, flung down the steps and pushed and dragged back into her cell.

The frog march, and the other assaults and cruelties, the brutal feeding by force, were resorted to while she was an unconvicted prisoner. Prison officials, encouraged by the Government, have cast aside both law and humanity in dealing with women political prisoners.

Source B: A letter written to a newspaper "The Dundee Advertiser," in 1913

To the Editor of the Dundee Advertiser.

Sir - I would suggest to the authorities that the next time the suffragettes decide to riot and disturb a public meeting the water hose should be turned upon them. A few firemen could be put behind the barricades, then when the "high-bred" hooligans, followed by a horde of low-bred hooligans, came surging along the firemen can simply cool their feverish frenzy and break no bones. The women would quickly melt away like the mist of the morning. No need for a hunger strike or mounted police. The cold water would cure them completely, and save the taxpayers a lot of expense.,

A.D., HOOLIGAN HATER

Source C: Adapted from an account of the 1984 Miners' Strike on a website.

Bitter disputes remain over the tactics used; the use of the Metropolitan Police in local mining villages, accusations of biased newspapers, flying pickets to discourage strike breakers from working. As the demonstrating grew there were violent confrontations between pickets and police. A key confrontation was the 'Battle of Orgreave' when one mass picket on 18th June 1984 was 10,000 strong and the pickets were met with police in riot gear, police horses and dogs. The strike also saw mass meetings and great marches where dockers and railway workers joined miners. However, opinion was divided about the violence and tragedies which occurred, for example the death of one flying picket and when a taxi driver died taking two 'scab' miners to work in South Wales, after a concrete post was dropped from a bridge onto his car.

Source D: An extract from a 2010 article by David Whetstone on journallive.co.uk reviewing the book *No Redemption* which looks at the difficulties faced by the families of miners during the strike.

History records that they did, indeed, get past Christmas. The union's area executive ensured that every family got a turkey and a tenner, but others rallied round to ensure miners' children didn't get overlooked by Santa.

The close-knit nature of the old mining communities ensured that nobody starved or froze. Marilyn remembered how she and other wives kept the kitchen going and also advised women in other mining areas how to get one started. She recalled many acts of support and generosity, from the old man who came in to put a fiver in the strike fund to the Durham University students who donated food.

Source E: A painting by John Bartlett of the Poll Tax riots in Trafalgar Square on 31 March 1990. The painting is now displayed in the Museum of London.

Source F: An account of the Poll Tax Riots by a demonstrator who was arrested.

Eyewitness account of Anti-poll Tax Riot

I arrived in Trafalgar Square to see riot police attacking demonstrators with batons and shields. But people were not taking it. They fought back with whatever they could find. One police officer got separated from his group. He was cornered by the theatre on Whitehall. Someone lifted the visor on his crash helmet and punched him in the face. He dropped. Then the police horses charged, supported by police vans. But the crowd was so big they could not force their way through.

Not long after that one of the buildings in Trafalgar Square was set on fire. The heat from the fire became so intense it was dangerous to stay in the square. I marched with about 2000 other demonstrators to Piccadilly Circus and then up Regent's Street. We wanted to get to the BBC to demand they broadcast the truth about the protest.

As we walked up Regent's Street all you could hear was the sound of breaking glass. Looters, young and old, smashed the huge plate glass windows of all the posh designer shops. Ordinary shoppers who hadn't even been on the demonstration joined in. It was a like a scene from a revolution. There was a jubilant atmosphere. We hated Thatcher and now the whole world knew it!

Inference and portrayal questions

Unit 3 tests your evidence skills by giving you an enquiry to carry out, based on a set of sources. You are expected to know something about the topic and that will help you to understand the sources, but you do not need to use your own knowledge in your answers until question 5.

Question 1: inference

In Unit 3, question 1 will usually be phrased: 'What can you learn from Source A about …?', This is an inference question and you answer it in exactly the same way as the inference question in Unit 2 (see page 6).

- You need to work out something that is not stated in the source – for example, people's attitude, the fact that something was difficult or an overall impression.

- You also need to show which bit of the source you have used to make that inference.

The only difference from Unit 2 is that in Unit 3 the inference question is worth 6 marks – therefore you need to make and support **TWO** inferences.

Everything else is the same as in Unit 2: there are no marks in the inference question for your own knowledge and you should not waste time writing long answers to this question. Although you are given two sides of the exam booklet to write your answer, you should really only need one side to make and support two inferences.

Question 2: portrayal

In Unit 3, question 2 is about portrayal – the way something is presented. The source can be a visual or a written source and the question can be worded in various ways. For example:

- how does the artist convey his message?

- what impression is created in Source B?

- why do you think this painting was done?

- how can you tell that the author of Source B disapproves of the situation?

Your answer should be focused on analysing the different elements of the source and showing how the selection and treatment of these details have been used to create a particular impression.

Analysing portrayal is all about identifying these individual elements and showing how they work together to create an overall impression.

How will I be marked?

Portrayal questions are worth 8 marks and the mark scheme has 3 Levels.

Level	Marks	Answer
1	1–2	The answer makes a valid comment about the message or portrayal in the source OR The answer writes about details from the source but does not link these to the message or impression created.
2	3–5	The answer makes a valid comment about the message or impression created and links this to details from the source.
3	6–8	The answer analyses the way the source details build up to create a message or impression either through the choice of details to include and leave out, or the treatment and way the detail is presented.

Level 3 answers need to focus on the choice of details to include and the way they are treated.

- In a visual source, this might mean that you comment on the way items or people are grouped in the picture, the way that light and colour are used to draw your attention, the expressions on people's faces and so on.

- In a written source, you should comment on the language used and the way that points are arranged – for example, does the author emphasise all the positive points and only cover negative ones very briefly at the end?

Things to avoid

If you're aiming to write a Level 3 answer, you need to make sure you leave enough time for the questions worth more marks. Focus on what you need to do and avoid wasting time on any of the points below.

- Lengthy descriptions of the source – focus on analysis.

- Evaluating the source for reliability – the mark scheme for portrayal questions gives no marks for this as it is covered in a separate question.

- Writing about the situation from your own knowledge – you're being asked about the impression created in **this** source.

3A The transformation of surgery c.1845–c.1918

In Unit 3A, the sources are all about developments in surgery during a key period (c.1845–c.1918). At the start of this period, operations were painful and often fatal, so people agreed to have surgery only when they were desperate. Because they were so painful, operations had to be carried out as quickly as possible; this meant that only basic operations could be carried out. The first question sometimes asks about the problems of surgery as a way of 'setting the scene' before you go on to look at changes.

Here is an example of an inference question (question 1):

> What can you learn from Source A about the way operations were carried out in the mid-nineteenth century? (6 marks)

Activity

1. Use Source A (page 68) to provide supporting evidence for the three inferences below.

There were spectators at many operations. I can work this out from the fact that ....

....

....

The conditions were unhygienic. This is shown by ....

....

....

The equipment was basic. This inference is supported by ....

....

....

2. Using the mark scheme on page 74, give Answer A a mark and explain your decision.

Answer A

In Source A there is a wooden table where the patient was held down while the operation was done. The surgeon's coat is hanging on the wall. There are also places for spectators to stand and watch. I can tell from Source A that operations were painful. They were so painful that operations had to be done as quickly as possible and the danger from infection and blood loss meant that people did not agree to have an operation unless they were desperate.

I would give this answer .... marks because ....

....

....

Now here is an example of a portrayal question (question 2):

> What impression of the anaesthetic is given in Source B? (8 marks)

Read Source B on page 68. First of all, think about how the selection of content to be included in the source and the omission of other details helps to create a specific impression. Then think about the treatment of that detail (the way it is organised or what is emphasised).

Now read Answer B below, which would be a Level 3 answer.

Answer B

Source B creates the impression that the anaesthetic is a new discovery and it is dangerous. The author says the assistant had 'just prepared a liquid which I thought worthy of experiment'. Saying 'just prepared' suggests that it was a brand new mixture and 'worthy of experiment' shows they hadn't tested it before. The idea that it was dangerous is shown by the way that the author insisted on trying it out on rabbits before letting Simpson test it and by the dramatic way he says that the rabbits had died.

3. Underline the places where Answer B shows how the choice of words creates an impression of the anaesthetic.

4. Circle the places where Answer B shows how the treatment of the detail creates an impression of the anaesthetic.

Activity

Here is another example of of a portrayal question (question 2):

> What impression of Simpson is given in Source B? (8 marks)

5. First of all, read Source B and decide which of the following words is most appropriate to describe the impression given of Simpson: curious/clever/daring/thoughtful.

6. Now explain how that impression is created by completing the following writing frame.

The source shows Simpson is .... by the use of words such as ....

....

....

This impression is backed up by the way it mentions ....

....

....

....

3B Protest, law and order

In Unit 3B the sources deal with one or more of four key protests in Britain during the twentieth century: the suffragettes, the General Strike, the Miners' Strike, and the Poll Tax protests. You will have looked at the causes, the leadership, the methods used by protestors and the results for each of these four case studies. You will also have learnt about how the authorities responded to these protests and the role of the economy, politics and the media in each of them. Some of the main issues you should think about are as follows:

- if the methods and tactics used by protestors helped them to achieve their aims or hindered them
- the various methods used by the authorities in dealing with protest
- the role of the media in influencing people's opinions about protest
- the impact that the economy and political issues may have had on the protest.

Here is an example of an inference question (question 1):

> What can you learn from Source A about how the authorities treated the suffragettes? (6 marks)

Activity

1. Use Source A on page 70 to provide supporting evidence for the three inferences below. Remember that your own knowledge will help you to understand the details you can see in Source A but your answer has to be based on the source.

The suffragettes were treated very harshly by the authorities. I can work this out from the fact that ....

....

....

The government was opposed to the suffragettes. This is shown by ....

....

....

The suffragettes were mistreated both physically and mentally by the authorities. This inference is supported by ....

....

....

2. Use the mark scheme on page 74 to assess Answer A overleaf and explain your decision.

Answer A

In Source A the suffragette was pulled by her hair and thrown so hard that her head hit the floor. Women were handcuffed and held in irons. The women were also force-fed and they were treated this way before they had been to court. The way they were treated by the prison staff was encouraged by the government.

I think Answer A is a Level .... answer because ....

....

....

Activity

Now here is an example of a portrayal question (question 2):

How can you tell that the author of Source B disapproves of the suffragettes? (8 marks)

Read Answer B below, which is a Level 3 answer.

Answer B

The author of Source B disapproves of the suffragettes. The source says that they were hooligans in quite large numbers and he uses the word 'horde.' This gives the impression that he thinks they are acting in an uncivilised manner. The author uses 'high-bred' in a sarcastic way to give the impression that the suffragettes think that they are high-class and well-bred but the author thinks that they are acting in a disrespectful way. He also shows how he thinks money should be saved and that taxpayers should be saved 'a lot of expense'.

3. Underline the places where Answer B shows how the choice of words creates an impression that the author disapproves of the suffragettes.

4. Circle the places where Answer B shows how the treatment of the detail creates an impression of disapproval of the suffragettes.

Cross-referencing questions

Question 3 in Unit 3 will usually ask you to examine how much the sources support a statement. The statement might be taken from one source and you are asked how far two other sources support it, or you might be asked to use three sources and reach a judgement on how far a given statement is supported by all three sources. There will always be points where the sources agree and points where they disagree.

How do I answer cross-referencing questions?

You will often have already used at least one of the sources in an earlier question but make sure you read them all carefully before answering this question.

When you are cross-referencing between sources, you need to look at these things:

> **Hint**
>
> Any question that asks 'how far' will require you to consider both sides of the issue before you make your judgement.

- how far the details of each source support or challenge the idea being tested

- how far the attitude or tone of the sources agree with the idea being tested

- how much weight to put on individual sources, so that you can weigh up the evidence on each side of the issue and come to a judgement.

How will I be marked?

This question is worth 10 marks, which are spread across three levels. The mark scheme below shows the criteria for Level 2 and Level 3.

Level	Marks	Answer
2	3–6	Answer matches the detail of the sources to find examples of support or challenge OR Answer evaluates sources for reliability.
3	7–10	Answer carefully analyses and weighs up the extent and importance of support and challenge between the sources OR Answer evaluates sources for reliability in order to consider the weight of each source as evidence.

There is no 'right' answer for these questions, but if you're aiming to write a Level 3 answer you have to consider the overall weight of the evidence on each side of the issue. Simply matching details between the sources is insufficient.

You should be prepared to spend at least five minutes going through all the details of each source and thinking about how much weight to place on the evidence before you write your answer. If you write a brief plan at this stage, you should only need another ten minutes to write a clearly structured and detailed answer.

Let's start by looking at an example question using just two sources:

> How far do Sources B and C suggest that Simpson deserves the credit for solving the problem of pain in surgery? (10 marks)

Activity

First read Answer A below, then look at the feedback that follows.

Answer A

Source B tells us how Simpson was willing to experiment on himself in an attempt to find an anaesthetic. He was so keen that he was prepared to try dangerous new mixtures even before they had been tested on animals. However, Source C tells us that Dr Robert Liston had used ether and found that it was an effective anaesthetic. He talks about it giving 'perfect and satisfactory results' and about how pleased he is that he has destroyed pain.

> This is a Level 1 answer – all it does is describe each source. There is a vague hint at the fact this point is not developed.

1. Below are two comments that could be added to Answer A to improve it. For each one, decide whether it would improve Answer A to a Level 2 or Level 3 answer and explain why.

Source B says Simpson was experimenting to find an anaesthetic which supports the idea that he deserves the credit for solving the problem of pain. However, Source C says Liston used ether, so this suggests that chloroform was not the only anaesthetic and therefore suggests that Simpson was not completely responsible for solving the problem of pain.

a) This would make the answer a Level .... answer because ....

....

....

Source B is very reliable. It comes from the Professor of Chemistry at Edinburgh University. He is talking about something he saw himself and the source suggests that he knew Simpson quite well and that Simpson did these experiments quite often. He has no reason to lie or exaggerate.

b) This would make the answer a Level .... answer because ....

....

....

Activity

It is always worth spending time planning your answer to the cross-referencing question.

2. Fill in the table below using Sources B and D to plan an answer comparing these two sources.

	Source B	Source D
Source content about Simpson and the discovery of anaesthetics		
Points of similarity		Simpson is shown as being very keen to solve the problem of pain and encourages others to use anaesthetics.
Points of difference		
Points about reliability		
How much weight can be placed on this evidence?		

3. Now put all this work together and, on a separate piece of paper, write an answer to the following question:

How far do Sources B, C and D suggest that Simpson deserves the credit for solving the problem of pain in surgery? (10 marks)

Let's start by looking at an example using two sources on the Poll Tax Riots:

> How far do sources E and F suggest that the protests became more violent because of the actions of the police? Explain your answer, using these sources. (10 marks)

Activity

First read Answer A and the feedback that follows it.

Answer A

Source F tells us that 'the police horses charged'. In Source E you can see the police attacking the protestors and they are in riot gear. All together these sources show that the police used a lot of force and violence in all the protests.

> This is a Level 1 answer – all it does is describe the content of each source, which is Level 1. It then matches the content of the three sources.

1. Below are two comments that could be added to Answer A to improve it. For each one, decide whether it would improve Answer A to a Level 2 or Level 3 answer and explain why.

Sources E and F agree with this because they describe both sides being violent. In Source F we are told about the protestors who 'smashed' and 'looters, young and old' and both the police and protestors are using violence in Source E. I think Source F particularly carries weight because it is an eye-witness account from a protestor who, whilst clearly being against the poll-tax, also gives examples of where the protestors were to blame for the violence.

This would make the answer a Level .... answer because ....

....

....

Source F tell us about how the protestors were also responsible for the protests becoming more violent. Also Source F tells us that the protestors 'fought back' and describes the looting and smashing up of expensive shops by the protestors. Source E also supports the view that it was both sides that were to blame as both the police and protestors appear to be using violence. Therefore it would seem that both the police and the protestors share some blame for the violence.

This would make the answer a Level .... answer because ....

....

....

It is always worth spending time planning your answer to the cross–referencing question.

2. Fill in the grid below using Sources E and F to plan an answer comparing these two sources.

	Source E	Source F
Source content about the police and the use of violence		
Points of similarity		
Points of difference		
Points about reliability		
How much weight can be placed on this evidence?		

Source evaluation questions

Question 4 in Unit 3 usually asks you to look at two sources and decide which is the more useful or valuable to the historian.

A source's usefulness or value depends partly on how much of the source content is relevant for the historian's enquiry. For example, a source may provide new detail about an event but not explain someone's motives for their actions or show people's attitudes. Another source might have less detail about what happened but give the historian a better understanding of how people felt. Equally important is the reliability of the source – can you trust the information? Ask yourself these questions:

- does the person who produced this source **know** the full truth?

- is the person who created this source **telling** the full truth?

How do I answer source evaluation questions?

Check the question carefully – what are you being asked to use the sources for? Is the historian investigating why an event happened, how important it was, or how people felt about it? The information in a source might be useful for one enquiry but not for another. Look at the content and see how the historian could use the information for the enquiry given in the question.

Then consider factors affecting reliability. Make sure you use any information you have been given in the source caption.

- The origins of the source might be important. Does it come from someone who should know what they're talking about? Is the source likely to be slanted towards a particular view? Was the source produced with hindsight – does the person perhaps want to justify what happened? Has it been produced by an historian who has researched both sides of an issue and can place it in a wider context?

- The nature and purpose of the source could also be relevant here. Diaries reflect the writer's personal feelings but are not always an accurate record of events. Some newspapers may sensationalise their accounts in order to please their readers but the basic facts should still be accurate.

- Look carefully at the language of the source. Do any of the words suggest the author has strong feelings on the issue?

- Does the source fit in with what you already know? Is it typical of the general situation, or just a single example that might create a false impression?

Remember
Reliability does **not** depend on how many details there are in the source (they could be made up) or whether it is a primary source (even eyewitness accounts are not automatically reliable as people may not know the full details).

A good answer can actually be quite short if it is well focused so it is worth making brief notes before you begin your answer. You could use a table like this one.

	Source A	Source B
Usefulness of source content		
Reliability		

How will I be marked?

This question is worth 10 marks and you should spend about 15 minutes on it.
The table below shows the criteria for Level 2 and Level 3 answers.

Level	Marks	Descriptor
2	4–7	Answer decides the value of the source by showing which source information helps the historian more OR by showing which source is more reliable.
3	8–10	Answer shows how the reliability of a source affects the value of the information it contains.

Notice that Level 3 answers must link reliability to the source content. The most important thing is to use the details of the source in your answer. Don't talk about a source being biased or exaggerated unless you can back it up with an example from the source. However, there is no 'right' answer. See the table on page 98 for examples of source evaluation.

Things to avoid

- Describing the source; you are are asked to evaluate it as evidence that could be used for an enquiry, you are not asked to actually carry out an enquiry.

- Assuming the source that tells you more must be better; it depends if the information is helpful for the enquiry.

- Making general comments that could apply to lots of sources; make your comments about this specific source.

- Making assumptions that sources from the time are reliable or that sources produced at a later date must be unreliable.

Activity

Read through the following question and Answer A.

> Which of Sources D and F is the most useful to the historian who is enquiring about people's reactions to Simpson's use of anaesthetics? (10 marks)

Answer A

Source D is very useful to the historian. It tells me that Dr Syme told the Medical Society of Edinburgh that he 'believed anaesthesia not only saved patients operated on from pain, but also from shock, and all its effects'. Dr Syme admits that at first he didn't believe Simpson about the benefits of chloroform but then he became convinced Simpson was right and used chloroform in all his operations after his first experiment. This source is very reliable. Dr Syme is talking about his own experiences so the details can be trusted. The fact that he admits that he didn't believe Simpson at first and then changed his mind also makes his view convincing.

1. Underline any points in Answer A which either:

   a) explains the value of **content**

   b) considers whether aspects of **reliability** strengthen or weaken the value of the source.

2. Read the feedback below, then explain why adding in the following two comments to Answer A would improve the answer to a Level 3 answer.

> The first part of this answer is Level 1 – it simply describes the source content, it doesn't say how that content is useful to the historian. The second part reaches Level 2 where it talks about reliability. (It would have been equally valid to say that Syme was trying to persuade the Medical Society about the benefits of chloroform, and so he might have over-emphasised the positive aspects and not mentioned any disadvantages.)

It is helpful to the historian because it shows the reasons why Dr Syme thought chloroform was an improvement in surgery.

....

....

The fact that Dr Syme was trying to convince other doctors about the importance of chloroform shows that his views were not typical and many doctors did not like anaesthetics.

....

....

3. Now complete a Level 3 answer by doing a similar analysis and evaluation for Source F:

Source F shows ....

....

This helps the historian who wants to know about people's reactions towards Simpson
and anaesthetics because ....

....

....

The source is a drawing of the event and therefore it is reliable/unreliable because ....

....

This affects the overall usefulness of the source because ....

....

....

Activity

4. Now try this further practice by reading through the list of sources below.

     a. A private letter from a surgeon to a friend after using Lister's antiseptic methods
       for the first time.

     b. An official record, e.g. hospital records of deaths after an operation before and
       after the use of antiseptics.

     c. An attack on Lister's methods, written by another surgeon.

     d. A history book called *Great Medical Discoveries*.

5. Explain which source would be best if the historian was trying to find out the reactions of
other surgeons to antiseptics.

....

....

6. Explain which source would be best if the historian was trying to decide how much
improvement in surgery there was after the use of antiseptics.

....

....

Activity

Read through the following question and Answer A.

> Which of Sources C and D is more useful to the historian who is enquiring into how united the miners were during the strike in 1984? Explain your answer, using Sources C and D. (10 marks)

Answer A

Both sources are useful because they are from interviews from people who were there and they all describe how they helped each other out and so it shows the miners were united. Source D tells us about how a miner's wife ran 'a kitchen for the strikers' and how they all supported others to make sure that at Christmas the children 'didn't get overlooked'. It also says the miners were 'close-knit' and how they 'advised women in other mining areas'. But it is only really details about one mining village and so we don't know about other parts of the country. Source D gives us examples of miners being united but it also says 'opinion was divided' and it gives an example of 'scab' miners so this shows they were not always united. Because it gives both sides of the argument it makes it more useful to the historian.

1. Mark up Answer A.

   a. Circle where the answer **explains** the value of the content detail.

   b. Underline where the answer **considers whether** aspects of reliability strengthen or weaken the value of the source.

2. Read the feedback below, then explain why adding in the following two comments to Answer A would improve it to a Level 3 answer.

> This answer is Level 2. It does not explain the value of the source content and does not link reliability to the content, and therefore it cannot get to Level 3.

Source D is useful to the historian because it gives us specific examples from a mining community from those that were there. However, these examples have probably been specifically chosen for a book with a specific purpose in mind.

....

....

Source C is useful because it shows us how complex the strike was. It gives details from the strike in different parts of the country and gives examples from both sides during the Miners' Strike.

....

....

3. Now complete a Level 3 answer by doing a similar analysis and evaluation for Sources C and D if you were enquiring about the amount of support that miners had from other groups of people.

Source C shows ....
....

This helps the historian looking at the amount of support that miners had because ....
....
....

Source D is reliable/unreliable because ....
....
....

This affects the overall usefulness of the source because ....
....
....

Activity

4. Look at the range of sources below.

a) Write the letter A next to the sources you would find useful to follow an enquiry into the effects of the strike on the lives of miners and their families.

b) Write the letter B next to the sources you would find useful to follow an enquiry into the response of the authorities to the miners' strike.

     A. A newspaper report which supported the government

     B. A newspaper report which supported the miners

     C. A BBC news report on the strike

     D. The diaries of a member of the government

     E. An interview with a police officer injured during the strike

     F. A map showing the different parts of the country where the miners were on strike

     G. A book called *Memories of a Mining Community*

     H. An interview with the wife of a retired miner

Judgement questions

Unit 3 is always based around an enquiry. The Background Information at the start of the Sources Booklet identifies the key issue and the final question in Unit 3 always asks you to make a judgement on that issue. This question carries 16 marks and it is very similar to the 16-mark questions in Unit 1 and Unit 2 (see pages 42–3). For example, it could be about the importance of a person or a factor, it could be about causes or consequences, it could be about change, and so on.

How do I answer judgement questions?

The question is often phrased as a statement and you are asked 'How far do you agree?' This should make you automatically plan an answer which looks at both sides – reasons for agreeing and reasons for disagreeing – but you still need to analyse the question in the same way as you would treat the questions in Units 1 and 2. For example:

- identify the topic

- check the time frame

- think about what angle or focus is expected.

The big difference is that Unit 3 is the source paper and therefore you need to use both your own knowledge and the specified sources in your answer. Own knowledge could be used to give extra detail about something mentioned in a source or to bring in a totally new point.

How will I be marked?

The mark scheme is very similar to the one used in Units 1 and 2 but look carefully at the requirements to **use the sources and your own knowledge**. An otherwise excellent answer can still struggle if it does not do so.

The table below gives the mark scheme for Level 3 and Level 4.

Level	Marks	Descriptor
3	9–10	Answer makes a judgement, showing how evidence from the sources or own knowledge supports or challenges that judgement.
	11–12	Answer makes a judgement, showing how evidence from **sources and own knowledge** supports or challenges that judgement.
4	13–16	Answer weighs the evidence **from sources and own knowledge** on both sides of the issue, showing clearly how the judgement has been reached.

Once again, there is no expected 'right' answer – the best answers look at both sides of the issue and support their judgement with evidence from the sources and own knowledge.

Spelling, punctuation and grammar

In question 5 there are up to 3 additional marks for spelling, punctuation and grammar. The table below shows how you will be marked.

Unit 3 Question 5	
0 marks	Errors severely hinder the meaning of the response or students do not spell, punctuate or use the rules of grammar within the context of the demands of the question.
Level 1: Threshold performance 1 mark	Students spell, punctuate and use the rules of grammar with reasonable accuracy in the context of the demands of the question. Any errors do not hinder meaning in the response. Where required, they use a limited range of specialist terms appropriately.
Level 2: Intermediate performance 2 marks	Students spell, punctuate and use the rules of grammar with considerable accuracy and general control of meaning in the context of the demands of the question. Where required, they use a good range of specialist terms with facility.
Level 3: High performance 3 marks	Students spell, punctuate and use the rules of grammar with consistent accuracy and effective control of meaning in the context of the demands of the question. Where required, they use a wide range of specialist terms adeptly and with precision.

3A The transformation of surgery

The best answers to this question have usually been carefully planned. It's a good idea to spend 5 minutes planning your answer before you start writing. This will ensure that your answer:

- covers both sides of the question

- uses the sources **and** your own knowledge

- builds up a clear argument and moves smoothly from point to point.

Activity

Read the following question:

> 'The development of anaesthetics was a major advance in surgery.'
> Explain how far you agree with this statement, using your own knowledge, Sources C, E and F and any other sources you find helpful. (16 marks)

1. Complete the planning table for this question (don't worry if you have to leave a box blank because all the points from a source seem to be on one side of the issue).

Evidence	Points to support the statement	Points to challenge the statement
Source C		
Source E		
Source F		
Own knowledge		

2. Now rearrange your evidence so that your essay has a logical structure to it by using the following plan.

Evidence to show that the development of anaesthetics was a major advance in surgery.

○ Source.............................Own knowledge ....

○ Source.............................Own knowledge ....

Evidence to show that the development of anaesthetics was not a major advance in surgery.

○ Source.............................Own knowledge ....

○ Source.............................Own knowledge ....

○ Your judgement ....

3. The following pairs of answers show common mistakes. The first answer in each pair is a typical Level 2 answer. In each case explain why Answer B is better and is a typical Level 3 or Level 4 answer.

Answer A
Source C says anaesthetics were a great advance in surgery.

Answer B
In Source C, Dr Liston obviously thinks anaesthetics were an advance in surgery as he says he had perfect results after using ether in a painful operation and he calls the use of anaesthetics 'a very great thing'

Answer B is better because ....

....

It would be a Level .... answer.

Answer A
Source E shows a problem in using chloroform.

Answer B
Source E shows a problem in using chloroform where the patient died from a small amount of chloroform. This was also shown when Hannah Greener died after receiving a small amount in her operation to remove a toenail.

Answer B is better because ....

....

It would be a Level .... answer.

Below is an extract from a student answer with a number of spelling, punctuation and grammar errors. Read the answer and then:

o underline any spelling mistakes

o circle any errors of punctuation or grammar

o rewrite the extract with accurate spelling, punctuation and grammar on a separate sheet of paper.

one of the main problems caused by anethetics were infection because surgens could perform more complex operations with anethetics and also operations were done for smaller problems as said in source x sepsis occurred. the use of anethetics in operations before anticeptics were developed is known as the black period of sergery due to high death rates, source x shows the problems of infection saying 'infection and gangrene spread through the wards'. also because more complex oparations occured the problem of blood loose became something that skilled many people, also doses were not decided on so many patents like hannah greener died on overdose, also ether and cloroform had problems, ether was extreamely flamable and irritated lungs and cloroform could stop the heart, also as source y shows the army were against using cloroform as they felt men should bite the bullet. on the other hand anethetics did improve sergery, as source z shows many patents would died from shock before anethetics so most people would not have operations, this is also in source w were it says the greatest danger was pain and some patents did not recover and anethetics offered hope to patents which suggests it was a benefit. overal I think that without anethetics sergery may not of developed to the modern tecniques used today like anticeptics as the high death rates would of prevented progress.

3B Protest, law and order

The best answers to this question have usually been carefully planned. It's a good idea to spend 5 minutes planning your answer before you start writing. This will ensure that your answer:

- covers both sides of the question

- uses the sources **and** your own knowledge

- builds up a clear argument and moves smoothly from point to point.

Activity

Look at the question below:

'For protestors the media was a useful way to gain support.' How far do you agree with this view? Explain your answer, using your own knowledge, Sources A, B, C and F and any other sources you find helpful. (16 marks)

1. Complete the planning table for this question (don't worry if you have to leave a box blank because all the points from a source seem to be on one side of the issue).

Evidence	Points to support the statement	Points to challenge the statement
Source A		
Source B		
Source C		
Source F		
Own knowledge		

2. Now rearrange your evidence so that your essay has a logical structure to it by using the following plan.

Evidence to show that the media was a useful way of gaining support.

○ Source .... Own knowledge ....

○ Source .... Own knowledge ....

Evidence to show the media was not a useful way to gain support.

○ Source .... Own knowledge ....

○ Source .... Own knowledge ....

○ Your judgement ....

3. The following pairs of answers show common mistakes. The first answer in each pair is a typical Level 2 answer. In each case explain why Answer B is better and is a typical Level 3 or Level 4 answer.

Answer A
Source A shows that newspapers were useful in getting people to know about how the suffragettes were treated badly.

Answer B
In Source A, the suffragettes are using a leaflet to spread their message and to get support. They include phrases like 'her face on the floor' and 'in this terrible state' to get sympathy from the reader.

a) Answer B is better because ....

....

....

Answer A
Source F tells us that poll tax protestors wanted to get on the television by getting to the BBC so that many people would know about the protest.

Answer B
Source F shows that the protestors wanted to get to the BBC. This was to get their views across and to make sure that 'the truth' was told. This shows us that some thought the BBC might not show their side of the story. This links with Source D where it says that during the Miners' Strike some thought there had been 'biased newspapers'.

b) Answer B is better because ....

....

....

Activity

Below is an extract from a student answer with a number of spelling, punctuation and grammar errors. Read the answer and then:

○ underline any spelling mistakes

○ circle any errors of punctuation or grammar

○ rewrite the extract with accurate spelling, punctuation and grammar on a separate sheet of paper.

during the miners strikes there was some cases of vilence like the battle of orgreave and a taxi driver killed when taking a miner to work. it was said in the battle of orgreve that the miners' used vilence against the police eg in source x it says police offisers were attacked with bricks, it is also implied in source w that miners using vilence and the bbc shown scens of miners' attacking police. a taxi driver was kill on the way to a pit when taking a working miner there, this made the public angry and resulted in miners loosing support from the public as they thought the miners was becoming too militent, this is also coroborated by source z as it shows how public opinion was firm against the miners. scabs were often beaten up and ostercised and this angered the public as they felt people shouldn't be beaten up purley for doing there job. years after the strikes the bbc admited that the minors did not attack the police first at orgreave and infact the bbc had broadcasted the events in the wrong order, this is coroborated by source y as it says the police charge provoked the missile throwing

Source Reliability

The table below outlines some of the strengths and weaknesses of different types of sources.

Source type	How reliability strengthens the value of the source content	How reliability weakens the value of the source content
Diary, letter	Personal source; no reason for the author to lie; can offer extra information from someone involved.	From one person's perspective; could exaggerate their own role or give a slanted view.
Newspaper, poster	Contains the key points; probably reflects public attitudes.	Presented in a certain way, e.g. using loaded language; can create a misleading impression.
Official records	Based on accurate facts; show the views of the government.	Details possibly selected or presented in a certain way to influence the public's attitude.
Photograph, newsreel or films from the time, etc.	Usually an accurate image; shows small details of clothes, objects, people's expressions, etc.	Can be posed or taken from a particular angle; literally a snapshot of one moment – does not show before/after; cannot tell if it shows a typical scene.
Drawing, painting, cartoon	Often indicate people's feelings and ideas.	Do not know if the details are true or imagined, or if it represents the general situation/attitude.
Book by an historian, official website	Secondary sources are based on a wide range of sources covering both sides of an issue and placing it in context; should be a very accurate source.	The historian could find it hard to agree with the views of the people at the time or his attitude to an event might be affected by his knowledge of what happened later.

Units 1 and 2

Inference: 1A Medicine through time (pages 7–8)

1 b) and d). Answer A is based on comment b).

2 Comment d) could be supported by explaining that the woman in Source A is working from a 'recipe' book whereas Source B says nurses carry out 'the treatment prescribed by a doctor'.

3–5 Read the feedback under Answer B.

6 Your improved answer should mention details in A showing the woman is nursing the man at home whereas Rathbone is writing in Source B to several nurses saying they are 'trained and skilled workers' suggesting there is a group of them – presumably at a hospital. Do not include the comment about Florence Nightingale, which is not based on the source.

Inference: 1B Crime and punishment (pages 9–10)

1 b) and d). Answer A is based on comment b).

2 Comment d) could be supported by the use of the word 'riot' in Source A and the claim it is 'necessary' to use military force suggests it is an emergency whereas in Source B the police already have the equipment which suggests it is normal duties.

3–5 Read the feedback under Answer B.

6 Your improved answer should mention the use of military force in A compared to the defensive wall that can be seen in Source B. You should not include the comment about police uniform, which is not based on the source.

Inference: 2B American West (pages 11–12)

1 d)

2 1B, 2A, 3B, 4B, 5B

3 Your answer should include a clearly supported inference from the source.

4 Answer A: 4 marks because the inference about the city being wealthy is supported directly from the source with reference to the size of the temple. Answer B: 0 marks because the response is the student's own knowledge and makes no use of the source at all.

5 You should have underlined the first two sentences. The answer does not need own knowledge about Brigham Young, the Perpetual Emigration Fund or the establishment of Utah.

Inference: 2C Life in Germany (pages 13–14)

1 b) and e)

2 1A, 2B, 3A 4B, 5B

3 Your answer should include a clearly supported inference from the source.

4 Answer A mark: 3 marks because there is a valid inference about a method of Nazi government's control with book-burnings, with "which they did not agree". The inferences about "busy areas" and "ceremony" could have been supported more directly from the source to give a 4 mark answer. Answer B: 0 marks because the response is the student's own knowledge and makes no use of the source at all.

5 You should have underlined the first three sentences. The answer does not need own knowledge about the Nazi government's policies on censorship.

Causation: 1A Medicine through time (pages 16–17)

1 You should have underlined the sentences starting: 'He felt it only had limited use…', 'It was also difficult to produce…', 'He published…' and 'They needed funding…'.

2 Row 1: Yes – shows that difficulty in mass production, combined with the fact that penicillin did not seem suitable for use as a medicine, meant it did not seem worthwhile trying to develop penicillin.

Row 2: Yes – explains that problems in purifying it in larger quantities created an added delay in finding ways to make it effective as medicine.

Row 3: Yes – shows it was difficult to get funding and without that funding it was difficult to develop the technology to mass produce penicillin.

Row 4: No - Tells us how penicillin was purified and mass produced but doesn't explain why that couldn't be done at an earlier date so this would not increase the marks for this answer even though the detail is correct.

3 …*ideas from different specialists could be pooled and new ideas suggested; people didn't repeat the same experiments.*

…*government funding made it possible to discover which method and equipment was most successful for purifying and mass production.*

…*war acted as a catalyst because the government now decided to provide funding in order to save lives.*

Causation: 1B Crime and punishment (pages 18–19)

1 You should have underlined the phrases: 'it was usually carried out in secret… in the dark', 'There were lots of different…too many to be watched', 'Also there was no police…catch the smugglers', 'people benefited from smuggling …authorities' and 'smugglers could also be very violent …authorities to catch the smugglers'.

2 Row 1: Yes - this suggests the combination of lots of places where smuggling could occur together with the limited number of officials made it difficult to catch smugglers.

Row 2: No – this tells us more about smuggling, not about why it was difficult to enforce the laws against it, so this would not increase the marks even though the detail is correct.

Row 3: Yes – this shows why people supported the smugglers and therefore would not help the authorities.

Row 4: Yes - shows that the various reasons why people would not act against the smugglers meant that the authorities had little help.

3 …*it was difficult for the small number of officials to spot the crime unless they were in the right place at the right time.*

…*poaching provided 'free' food for poor families and many liked that they could afford to buy luxury goods from smugglers.*

…*people felt these crimes didn't hurt anyone and even their social superiors bought things from smugglers.*

Causation: 2B American West (pages 20–21)

1 a) A and B

Causation: 2C Life in Germany (pages 22–23)

1 A and B

Consequence: 1A Medicine through time (pages 25–26)

1 Not relevant: 1 & 5. Relevant: 2, 3 & 4.

2 Points 2 and 3 about the books of Vesalius and Harvey provide examples to support the comment in the first sentence. Point 4 has some added details that could be included in the final sentence of the answer.

Consequence: 1B Crime and punishment (pages 27–28)

1 Not relevant: 1 & 5. Relevant: 2, 3 & 4.

2 Point 2 supports the comment in the first sentence about the ideas of reformers and the purpose of punishment. Points 3 and 4 show her ideas influencing other people.

Consequence: 2B The American West (pages 29–30)

1 A: There were almost 100,000 in California by 1849..

B: These shanty towns grew up very quickly.

C: The early mining towns were very lawless and systems of law and order needed to be put in place.

D: Gold supplies ran out in California and there were later discoveries in the Rocky Mountains and the Black Hills.

E: Men migrated to California from other parts of America and from Europe.

F: California became part of the route of the first transcontinental railroad.

G: Discoveries of gold were important in the US playing a major role in world trade.

2 Social effects: 'The Forty-niners', Mining Towns, migration.

Economic effects: Later discoveries of gold, railroads, US economy.

Political effects: Law and order.

3 Short term effects: "The Forty-niners", mining towns, law and order, migration.

Long term: mining towns, law and order, later discoveries of gold, US economy.

5 Your statements might cover some of the following: the 1868 Fort Laramie Treaty, the US government's "small reservation" policy, General Custer's search for gold, claims to Sioux land, the US government's offer to buy the Black Hills, the Battle of Little Big Horn in 1876.

Consequence: 2C Life in Germany (pages 31–32)

1 A: Many suffered badly because their pensions became worthless.

B: Many lost their savings.

C: Some made money because the price of food went up.

D: It was hard to pay for basic goods as prices rose quickly.

E: Many benefitted as loans could be paid off quicker

F: Often owned property and land which did not lose value

G: Some could get access to cheap credit and take over businesses

2 Social effects: Hard to pay for goods, elderly suffered.

Economic effects: farmers, those in debt and some businessmen gained.

Political effects: led Hitler to try and achieve power in Munich Putsch.

3 Short term effects: businesses going bankrupt, people unable to buy basic goods.

Long term: how people voted.

5 Your statements might cover some of the following: trial of van der Lubbe, blamed by Hitler on the Communist Party, increase in public hysteria of a communist plot, arrests of Communists, passing of Emergency Decree, increase in Nazi share of vote in March 1933 election.

Role: 1A Medicine through time (pages 34–35)

1 The answer is Level 2 because it describes examples of science and technology in medicine but doesn't show how they improved medical understanding and why they were important.

2 Pasteur's work meant scientists understood what caused disease and therefore could look for effective treatment.

Technology helps doctors see what is happening inside the body and find problems such as tumours, which means they can understand and try to treat the exact cause of a problem.

We still can't treat or prevent genetic conditions but understanding what causes them is the first step.

Having drugs such as penicillin to cure illness is only good if they can be produced in large quantities, so technology is important.

3 1D, 2A, 3E, 4B, 5C.

Role: 1B Crime (pages 36–37)

1 Answer A is Level 2 because it gives lots of examples of technology being used but doesn't explain whether this improved the situation or how important the change was.

2 Technology has made some new crimes easier to commit or more difficult for the police to stop.

Technology has created new crimes which the police now have to find ways to deal with.

Technology has improved some police methods and made it easier to catch criminals.

3 1E; 2D; 3B; 4C; 5A

Role: 2B The American West (pages 38–39)

1 They are about problems facing homesteaders and are not made relevant to the question about 'the contribution of women'.

2 From "*But in many ways*" onwards clearly relates to the contribution of women to the white settlement of the Plains.

6 Turkey Red wheat and wind pumps are outside the time span of this question.

Role: 2C Nazi Germany (pages 40–41)

1 They are outside the time span of this question as they are not about Goebbels' role as Minister of Enlightenment and Propaganda.

2 From "Goebbels was very good at his job" onwards

6 The Wall Street Crash, Munich Putsch and *The Eternal Jew* are outside the time span of this question.

Evaluation: 1A Medicine through time (pages 44–47)
1 See feedback.

3 B

Evaluation: 1B Crime and punishment (pages 48–51)
1 See feedback.

3 B

Evaluation: 2B American West (pages 52–55)
1 "'Therefore" to "this changed their lives."; "As a result" to "move from Texas" and "Consequently" to "states far away."

2 *1866 the first cattle trail; American Civil War; 5 million; northern states; John Iliff; Texas Longhorns; Glidden invented barbed wire; 1869 completion of the first trans-continental railroad.*

3 *Donner Party; Manifest Destiny; Far East; San Francisco*

4 The first five lines on wagon trains could be reduced to a shorter explanation.

5 This would include details on the impact the railroads had on the lives of homesteaders and also led to a higher demand for more agricultural produce.

6 A; C; D; E; F; B

7 The first paragraph is Level 3. The last section from "therefore" shows a Level 4 judgement but more detailed support would be needed.

Evaluation: 2C Life in Germany (pages 56–59)
1 "This made it" to "look after children."; "This shows how" to "got married."; "This shows us" to "1000 year Reich."; "This meant that the government" to "also work."

2 *1,000 marks; 200 marks; pure Aryan; 3Ks; four for bronze and so on.*

3 *One day boycott; Nuremberg Laws; von Rath; Lebensraum; Einsatzgruppen; Warsaw; Wannsee; Final Solution; SS officers; death marches.*

4 The first four lines are outside the time frame of this question.

5 This would include details on how the Second World War changed Nazi policies towards the Jews and the reasons why more extreme methods were used

6 D; C; E; A; F

7 The first paragraph is Level 3 and the second paragraph makes it a Level 4 answer.

Unit 3
Inference and portrayal: 3A Surgery (pages 75–76)
1 …the room has space organised for a number of people to watch.

… the fact that people are wearing ordinary clothes, there are no surgical gloves or gowns, the instruments are washed, not sterilised.

… the fact that ordinary knives are used, there is limited equipment because people are needed to hold the patient down.

2 Answer A is 1 mark because it describes the room without making an inference, and the comments about pain, speed and infection cannot be supported from the source.

3 The phrase 'worthy of experiment' and the sentence 'Saying 'just prepared'' to 'tested it before' show how words create the impression chloroform was new.

4 The sentence 'The idea that it was dangerous' to 'rabbits had died' shows how the author used details to suggest that chloroform was dangerous.

5 'Curious' could be supported by the way Simpson is so keen to try out the new mixture. 'Daring' could be supported by the way Simpson wants to rush eagerly and not think about whether the mixture is dangerous.

Inference and portrayal: 3B Protest (pages 77–78)

1 … the source says this suffragette was 'thrown down,' her 'hair was seized' and her 'head bumping on the stairs.' She was also subjected to 'forcible feeding,' was 'handcuffed again' and 'flung down the steps.'

… the source saying that the prison authorities were 'encouraged by the government.'

… any examples about how they were treated.

2 Answer A is Level 2 as it makes a valid comment with details from the source.

3 From 'this gives' to 'in a disrespectful way'

4 From 'high-bred in a sarcastic way' to 'a lot of expense'

Cross referencing: 3A Surgery (pages 80–81)
1 a) Level 2 because it explains why the information is the source is useful to the historian.

b) Level 2 because it considers the reliability of the information.

2 Source content: B– Simpson didn't create chloroform; Simpson tested chloroform. D– Simpson suggested chloroform be used in operations. Dr Syme said Simpson was right, that it prevented pain and saved patients from shock.

Similarity: B– Simpson is experimenting to find a way of relieving pain. D– Simpson is shown as being very keen to solve the problem of pain and encourages others to use anaesthetics.

Difference: B– Simpson used other people's ideas. D– Simpson is given the credit for the use of anaesthetics.

Reliability: B– Speaking from personal knowledge, no reason to lie. D– Speaking from personal knowledge, has added weight because admits he changed his mind but was trying to persuade others to use chloroform as well.

How much weight: B– a lot. D– Quite a lot but perhaps doesn't know how Simpson discovered chloroform, just knows Simpson tried to get surgeons to use it.

Cross referencing: 3B Protest (pages 82–83)
1 This is Level 3 because it explains how the reliability of the source affects the value of the information it contains

This is Level 2 because it matches details from the sources to find examples of support

2 Source content: Source E – A painting of the Poll Tax riots in Trafalgar Square showing the police and rioters attacking each other. Source F - A description of the fighting between the police and protestors and details of what happened elsewhere.

Points of similarity: Source E - Both the protestors and police are using violence, there is a police van, a fire bomb going off and the police are using batons, shields and horses. Source F - Says the police are attacking and the rioters are fighting back using batons, shields and had horses.

Points of difference: Source E – This is only about what happened in Trafalgar Square and you can't tell who is the most to blame for the violence. Source F - Gives the impression that the rioters were fighting back but it also includes details about other things the protestors did outside of Trafalgar Square such as looting shops and smashing windows.

Points about reliability: Source E - The artist does not seem to be supporting either the police or the protestors. Source F - An eye-witness account from personal knowledge. A demonstrator might give a non-balanced view but it does include the violence of both the police and demonstrators.

How much weight: Source E - some weight, but we do not know enough about the person who made the picture. Source F - quite a lot of weight as it is from a protester with personal knowledge but with added weight as it gives details of actions by both sides.

Source evaluation: 3A Surgery (pages 86–87)
1 a) Nothing should have been underlined. The two sentences *'It tells me that Dr Syme…'* to *'…after his first experiment.'* describe the content but don't say how it helps the historian in his enquiry.

b) Two sentences should have been underlined – *'Dr. Syme is talking about…'* to *'…his view convincing'.*

2 The first comment explains why the information in the source is helpful to the historian.

The second comment gives an added point about the value of the source by considering whether it is a typical view.

3 *…people coming to see a statue of Simpson being unveiled.*

… it suggests many people admired him and wanted to honour him.

… it is unreliable because we do not know if details are accurate, such as the size of the crowd.

… we cannot assume from the picture that he was widely admired without knowing if the size of the crowd is accurate.

4 A private letter from a surgeon after using Lister's antiseptic methods is best for showing the reactions of surgeons to antiseptics because he can speak from experience and from his knowledge of other doctors' views.

5 Hospital records of changes in the number of patients who died after surgery is best for showing the improvement in surgery after antiseptics, because it is factual and not affected by personal views.

Source evaluation: 3B Protest (pages 88–89)
1 a) *'interviews from people that were there'* and *'gives both sides of the argument'*

  b) *'only really details from one mining village'*

2 Both comments show how reliability affects the value of the information in the source.

3 *… us that there was some support for the miners*

 … mass meetings, marches and the numbers of pickets as well as lack of support by mentioning 'scabs'. It shows both examples of support and lack of support.

… is partly reliable as it gives accounts from people that were there but it is only one side of the story.

… it is only from one mining village and is written for a book with a specific purpose.

4 a) B; E; H

  b) A; C; D; E

Judgement: 3A Surgery (pages 92–93)
1 Source C: Support: In both operations perfect and satisfactory results.

Challenge: Only two examples – not enough to support the claim that it was a major advance in surgery.

Source E: Support: Operation was painful so surgeon wanted to use chloroform – expected it to help.

Challenge: Difficult to be exact about dosage; patient had a stroke and died.

Source F: Support: Statue of Simpson shows people felt he deserved honour; crowd suggests he was admired.

Challenge: No information given to say who chose to erect the statue – doesn't necessarily show public opinion, or it could be in recognition of something else he did.

Own knowledge: Support: Explanation of the amount of pain felt, need for patient to be held down, need for speed, surgery as a last resort, only quick and 'easy' operations could be done.

Challenge: Lack of knowledge about germs led to Black Period when death rate actually increased; problem of blood loss remained so still needed to be quick.

3 In each case, Answer B is better because it combines detail from the source with additional own knowledge to support the point being made.

Judgement: 3B Protest (pages 95–96)
1 Source A: Points to support – *The suffragettes used leaflets to spread their opinions.*

Source B: Points to challenge – *This is a letter to a newspaper to try and raise opposition to the suffragettes.*

Source C: Points to challenge – *The mention of biased newspapers.*

Source F: Point to support – *The protestors wanted the BBC to put their point of view across.*

3 a) Answer B is better because it gives evidence directly from the source.

b) Answer B is better because it gives evidence directly from the source.